Edward J. Molloy

Handbook of Cook County institutions :

Review of its Business Transactions and Financial Affairs for Year 1895

Edward J. Molloy

Handbook of Cook County institutions :
Review of its Business Transactions and Financial Affairs for Year 1895

ISBN/EAN: 9783744770224

Printed in Europe, USA, Canada, Australia, Japan

Cover: Foto ©Andreas Hilbeck / pixelio.de

More available books at **www.hansebooks.com**

HAND BOOK

...OF...

COOK COUNTY INSTITUTIONS

REVIEW OF ITS BUSINESS TRANSACTIONS AND FINANCIAL AFFAIRS FOR YEAR 1895.

PUBLISHED UNDER THE SUPERVISION OF PRESIDENT D. D. HEALY.
COMPILED AND EDITED BY H. B. MEYERS.

CHICAGO:
PRESS OF WM. C. HOLLISTER & BRO.
1896.

Fenton Metallic Manufacturing Co.

Main Office and Factories: JAMESTOWN, N. Y.
CHICAGO OFFICE: Suite 688-9 Palmer House.

MANUFACTURERS OF HIGH GRADE CABINET WORK IN METAL

ESPECIALLY FOR PUBLIC BUILDINGS

ITS SPECIALTIES ARE:

METALLIC FIRE-PROOF FIXTURES FOR RECORD AND FILING ROOMS.

BOOK STACKS FOR LIBRARIES, ENTIRELY OF STEEL.

INTERIOR FIXTURES FOR VAULTS.

INCLUDING

Suspension Document Files for Folded Papers,

Files for Letters and Flat Papers,

Plain and Roller Book Shelving,

Drawer and Cupboard Bases.

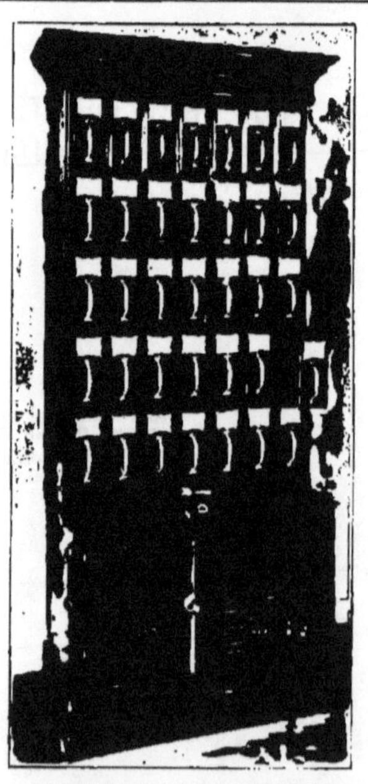

COMBINATION FILING CASE.

Its product embraces every form of Metallic Filing Device, together with Tables, Desks, Counters, Mantels in Steel and Bronze, and a general line of Cabinet Work in Metal.

The Company, having the largest plant in the world devoted exclusively to these lines, and a large experience in the equipment of rooms designed for the safe custody of Records, feels qualified not only to undertake the manufacture of such equipments, but to offer valuable suggestions as to their plan and arrangement.

FENTON METALLIC MFG. CO.

HAND BOOK

...OF...

Cook County and Its Institutions

REVIEW OF ITS BUSINESS TRANSACTIONS AND FINANCIAL AFFAIRS.

Aside from a comparatively small number of officials, it is safe to say that very few of the citizens of Chicago possess any practical knowledge of the extent or magnitude of the responsibilities which rest upon the shoulders of the officials of Cook County. These responsibilities lie primarily with the Board of County Commissioners, whose chief executive, President D. D. Healy, stands in a dual capacity as a representative of the people's interests and as the official administrator of county affairs. It is the purpose of this publication to present to the public a concise and reliable exhibit of the business transactions of the county, showing how the vast sums of money required for maintaining the county institutions are raised and how expended, giving in detail the reports of county officials, chiefs of departments, wardens of hospitals, clerks of the various courts, together with the routine observed in the transaction of business in the sheriff's office, the recorder's office, and all other bureaus and departments of the county service.

This is the first attempt that has been made to include in one volume a complete guide or index of the financial and official affairs of Cook County, and the work will be of decided interest to the citizen who desires to familiarize himself with public affairs, and will be of inestimable value to contractors, business houses and attorneys, and to that ever increasing class whose business frequently leads them to the courts or to one of the county institutions. The financial exhibits will be especially valuable, as they will set forth clearly and distinctly the resources and liabilities of the county.

This work is presented to the public in the most attractive typographical manner possible. The letter press is artistic; the paper heavy, finely finished and serviceable; the whole embellished with half-tone engravings representing the finest workmanship attainable, and as it will be used as a ready-reference book by a large and interesting class of citizens, experienced advertisers will readily recognize its value as a medium through which to reach the public. Care has been taken to present advertisements in a neat and attractive manner, and the work will be given a wide circulation in the homes and offices of Chicago's business and professional men. It will also be distributed in the public departments of the larger counties and cities throughout the United States.

GOODYEAR RUBBER CO.

141 LAKE STREET.

High Grade Work Done Quickly

Main Office, 144 22d Street

PHONE SOUTH 168.

Wagons Call Everywhere.

H. J. MERRIELL. GEO. H. MERRIELL.

MERRIELL BROS.

MANUFACTURERS, WHOLESALE AND RETAIL DEALERS IN

Stoves, Tin and Hardware

ALL KINDS OF

MILKMEN'S WARE, HOUSE FURNISHING GOODS, ETC.

214 South Halsted Street,

...CHICAGO...

Particular Attention Paid to Job Work.

BOARD OF COMMISSIONERS

...OF...

COOK COUNTY, ILLINOIS

FOR 1895-96

DANIEL D. HEALY, President and ex-officio member of all committees, 205 Court House. Residence Telephone Canal 176.

T. N. JAMIESON, Superintendent of Public Service, 205 Court House. Telephone Main 2968.

PHILIP KNOPF, County Clerk, Comptroller, Clerk of County Board, and Clerk of County Court, Court House, first floor, north end. Telephone Main 695.

JAS. L. MONAGHAN, Deputy County Comptroller and Clerk Board of County Commissioners, 210 Court House. Telephone Main 15.

E. J. MCARTHY, Chief Clerk Comptroller's office.

LESLIE H. MILLER, Chief Clerk Supt. of Public Service office.

COMMITTEE ON PUBLIC SERVICE.

John N. Cunning, Chairman, Office, 1482 Ogden Ave., 120 DeKalb St.
Oscar D. Allen, . . . Oak Park.
Henry J. Beer, . . Blue Island.
Chas. Burmeister, . 303 Larrabee St.
Daniel D. Healy, . 205 Court House.
Theo. W. Jones, 6655 Wentworth Ave.
Gustav W. Kunstman, 471 S. Paulina St.
John A. Linn, . 14 Clybourn Ave.
Thomas J. McNichols, 284 S. Loomis St.
Louis H. Mack, . . 824 Grand Ave.
David Martin, 168 Exchange Bldg., S.Y.
James M. Munn, ... Evanston.
John Ritter, . . 477 Wabash Ave.
Geo. Struckman, ... Bartlett.
Geo. D. Unold, . . . La Grange.

STANDING COMMITTEES

FINANCE

Allen, *Chairman*
Struckman Martin Mack Unold

ROADS AND BRIDGES

Beer, *Chairman* Unold Munn

SUB-COMMITTEES

INSANE ASYLUM.

Unold, *Chairman*
Ritter Linn McNichols Mack

COUNTY HOSPITAL

Munn, *Chairman*
Mack Burmeister Jones Struckman

OUT-DOOR RELIEF

Jones, *Chairman*
Linn Kunstman Munn Beer

JAIL AND CRIMINAL COURT

Linn, *Chairman*
McNichols Unold Martin Burmeister,

COURT HOUSE

Martin, *Chairman*
Struckman Ritter Mack Beer

CORONER AND MORGUE

Struckman, *Chairman*
Kunstman McNichols Beer Burmeister

BUILDING

McNichols, *Chairman*
Unold Martin Linn Ritter

JUDICIARY

Burmeister, *Chairman* Jones Munn

EDUCATION

Ritter, *Chairman* Kunstman Linn

STATIONERY AND PRINTING

Mack, *Chairman* Martin McNichols

CITY RELATIONS

Kunstman, *Chairman* Struckman Jones

CARSON, PIRIE, SCOTT & CO.

Wholesale

Dry Goods

NEW YORK, 115 Worth St.
MANCHESTER, 58 Portland St.
CHEMNITZ, 1 Neefe St.
PARIS, Rue d' Uzes 4.

ADAMS AND FRANKLIN STREETS

Chicago...

We offer immense stocks of desirable Merchandise and are at all times prepared to contract for the delivery of large quantities at the lowest possible prices.

CARSON, PIRIE, SCOTT & CO.

E. HELDMAIER & CO.

CUT STONE CONTRACTORS

... YARDS AND WORKS ...
AT
NORTHWEST COR. MAIN AND COLOGNE STREETS.

Yard Telephone, Canal 250

... CITY OFFICE ...

910 SECURITY BUILDING, ... MADISON AND FIFTH AVE.

Telephone Main 330.

COMMISSIONERS' DISTRICTS.

FIRST DISTRICT. CHICAGO.

Chas. Burmeister,	First District.	John A. Linn, . . .	First District.
John N. Cunning,	"	Thomas J. McNichols, .	"
Daniel D. Healy, .	"	Louis H. Mack, . .	"
Theodore W. Jones,	"	David Martin, .	"
Gustav W. Kunstman,	"	John Ritter, .	"

SECOND DISTRICT.—Towns of Barrington, Bloom, Bremen, Calumet, Cicero, Elk Grove, Evanston, Hanover, Hyde Park, Jefferson, Lake, Lake View, Lemont, Leyden, Lyons, Maine, New Trier, Niles, Northfield, Norwood Park, Orland, Palatine, Palos, Proviso, Rich, Riverside, Schaumberg, Thornton, Wheeling and Worth.

Henry J. Beer,	Second District.	Oscar D. Allen, .	Second District.
James M. Munn,	"	George Struckman, .	"
George D. Unold,	"		

County Officers and Heads of Departments.

Jacob J. Kern, . . .	State's Attorney.
James Pease, . . .	Sheriff.
D. H. Kochersperger, . .	County Treasurer.
Samuel B. Chase, . .	Recorder.
Frank J. Gaulter, . .	Clerk Circuit Court.
Stephen D. Griffin, . .	Clerk Superior Court.
Abijah O. Cooper, .	Clerk Probate Court.
Ernest J. Magerstadt, . .	Clerk Criminal Court.
James McHale, . . .	Coroner.
Orville T. Bright, .	County Supt. of Schools.
James D. Morrison, . .	Civil Service Commissiouer.
Edward D. Northam, .	Civil Service Commissioner.
Samuel M. Burdett, .	Civil Service Commissioner.
Geo. C. Waterman, .	County Surveyor.
Robt. S. Iles, .	County Attorney.
F. L. Shepard, . .	1st Asst. County Attorney.
Wm. F. Struckman, .	2d Asst. County Attorney.
Wm. H. Ward, . . .	3d Asst. County Attorney (tax matters.)
Dr. T. N. Jamieson, . .	Supt. Public Service.
Edward Austin, . .	Committee Clerk.
James H. Graham, . .	Warden County Hospital.
Geo. F. Morgan, . .	Supt. County Institutions, Dunning.
Dr. E. C. Fortner, .	County Physician.
Geo. S. Oleson, .	County Agent.
E. A. Bothne, . . .	Chief Jury Clerk.
S. B. Jamieson, . . .	County Electrician.
Frank Wimmerslage, .	County Farmer.
Warren H. Milner, .	County Architect.
Henry Bartels, . .	Custodian Court House.
Chris Dahnke, . .	Custodian Criminal Court Bldg.

THE WERNER COMPANY

160-174 ADAMS STREET, CHICAGO, ILL.

LARGEST PUBLISHING HOUSE IN THE WORLD

Controls the best and most varied line of Standard and Successful Subscription Books Published, Embracing

EDUCATIONAL WORKS, HISTORIES, BIOGRAPHIES, WORKS OF REFERENCE AND GENERAL LITERATURE.

SPECIALTIES:

THE ENCYCLOPEDIA BRITANNICA

Ninth Edition, with American Revisions and Additions.

PRINTERS, BINDERS AND LITHOGRAPHERS SUBSCRIPTION BOOKS.

MANUFACTURING PLANT AT AKRON, OHIO.

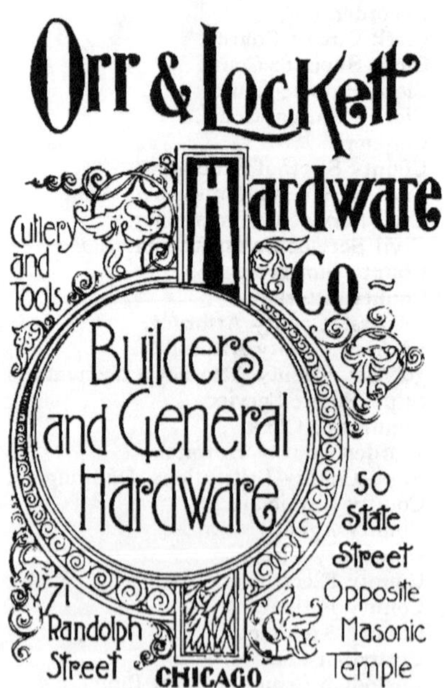

ECLIPSE

PEERLESS

AND

WASHINGTON

BICYCLES

DROP IN AND SEE 'EM

DIRECTORY OF COOK COUNTY COURT HOUSE
AND
CRIMINAL COURT BUILDING.

March 1st, 1896.

Room Directory, COOK COUNTY COURT HOUSE, Washington, Clark and Randolph Sts.

BASEMENT FLOOR.

5 Recorder's Chief Clerk.
7 Recorder's Receiving Department.
11 Recorder's Abstract Department.
19 Recorder's Examining Department.
25, 29, 31 } Sheriff's Offices.

2, 4, 6, 10 } Recorder's Folio Writers.
14 Carpenter Shop.
16 Engine Room.
28, 30 } Recorder's Map Department.

FIRST FLOOR.

County Clerk, north half of building. County Treasurer, south half of building.
Plumber of the building, west of elevators.

SECOND FLOOR.

203 President Board County Commissioners.
205 Superintendent Public Service.
207 Judge Windes.
213 Judge Windes, chambers.
217 Clerk County Court.
225 Clerk Circuit Court.
229 Circuit Court File Room.

200 Jury Room.
202 County Board Committee Room.
204 County Board Committee Clerk.
206 County Board Assembly Room.
208 Comptroller, private.
210 Comptroller's Office.
212 Judge Dunne, chambers.
214 Judge Dunne.
216 County Map Department.
218 Custodian of the Building.
226 Clerk Superior Court.

THIRD FLOOR.

301 Assistant County Attorney.
303 Judge Hutchinson, chambers.
307 Judge Hutchinson.
309 Cook County, Civil Service Commission.
313 Store Room.
317 Judge Carter, County Court.
321 Judge Carter, chambers.
323 Judge Adams, chambers.
327 Judge Adams.
331 Judge Neely, chambers.
333 Judge Neely.

302 Judge Gibbons, chambers.
306 Judge Goggin.
308 Judge Goggin, chambers.
310 Branch, County Court.
312 Judge Baker, chambers.
314 Judge Baker.
316 Judge Burke.
318 Judge Burke, chambers.
320 Recorder Torrens Land Title Department.
322 Judge Clifford, chambers.
326 Judge Clifford.

FOURTH FLOOR.

401 Circuit Court, Chancery Record Writers.
403 Chief Bailiff and Jury Clerk.
405 Superior Court Record Writers.
407 Judge Stein.
411 Judge Stein, chambers.
411 Judge Brentano, chambers.
413 Judge Brentano.
417 Judge Horton.
417A Judge Horton, chambers.
421 Judge Paine.
423 Judge Paine, chambers.
423 Judge Tuley, chambers.
427 Judge Tuley.

402 Judge Ewing, chambers.
404 Jury Room.
406 Judge Ewing.
408 Judge Hanecy.
410 Judge Hanecy, chambers.
414 Law Institute.
420 Clerk Probate Court, private.
422 Stairs to Attic.
424 Judge Kohlsaat, chambers.
426 Judge Kohlsaat, Probate Court.
428 Clerk Probate Court.

HENRY BARTELS, Custodian Court House.

DIRECTORY OF CRIMINAL COURT BUILDING.

Dearborn Ave. and Washington St.

1st floor, left or west side, Clerk of Criminal Court.
1st " right or east " Sheriff's Office.
1st " right or east " Coroner's office.
2d " left or west " State's Attorney's Office.
2d " right or east " Branch 1, Criminal Court.
3d " left or west " " 2, " "
3d " right or east " " 3, " "
4th " left or west " " 4, " "

4th floor, left or west side, Custodian of Building.
4th " right or east " Branch 5, Criminal Court.
5th " left or west " Judge Sears, Superior "
5th " right or east " Judge Freeman " "
5th " office of Asst. County Attorney Struckman.
6th " left or west side, Branch 6, Criminal Court.
6th " right or east " Grand Jury Room.
6th " right or east " Asst. State's Att'y Office.

CHRIS. DAHNKE, Custodian of Criminal Court Building.

W. R. THOMPSON

..PLUMBING AND GAS FITTING..

IRON AND TILE SEWERING.

FINE RESIDENCE WORK A SPECIALTY.
JOBBING PROMPTLY ATTENDED TO.

85 EAST LAKE STREET,

TELEPHONE MAIN 636.

TREMONT HOUSE BASEMENT.

P. F. PETTIBONE & Co. (INC.)

48-50 JACKSON STREET, 46-50 SOUTH DESPLAINES STREET,

LAW AND PUBLIC OFFICE STATIONERS,
PRINTERS, LITHOGRAPERS, BLANK BOOK MAKERS,
NATIONAL CABINET LETTER FILES.

AMPLE FACILITIES FOR EXECUTING PROMPTLY
LARGE PRINTING CONTRACTS.

—THE—

PROVIDES FOR ITS PATRONS

EVERY Accommodation and Comfort Known to Modern Railroading.

LUXURIOUS Parlor and Dining Cars by Day
PALACE Buffet Sleeping Cars by Night.

Solid Vestibuled Trains Daily Between Chicago Cincinnati And All Points South
Indianapolis Louisville

Heated by Steam. Illuminated by Pintsch Light.

ONLY LINE TO THE FAMOUS HEALTH RESORTS

West Baden and French Lick Springs

"THE CARLSBAD OF AMERICA"

HOTELS OPEN THE YEAR ROUND.

W. H. McDOEL,
Vice-President and General Manager.

FRANK J. REED,
General Passenger Agent.

GENERAL OFFICES: 198 Custom House Place,
CHICAGO

DANIEL D. HEALY,
President Board of Commissioners, Cook County, Ill.

.. THE ..

GUTTA PERCHA & RUBBER MFG. CO.

JOHN H. BROWN, Manager.

IN

NEW LOCATION

96 AND 98 LAKE STREET, .. CORNER DEARBORN STREET,

ARE IN A POSITION TO GIVE ORDERS FOR

RUBBER GOODS

THE BEST POSSIBLE ATTENTION.

ESTABLISHED IN CHICAGO 12 YEARS.

HEBARD'S... Telephones West 283 and 053.

Tally-Ho Coaches

Band Wagons and Omnibusses

For PARTIES...PARADES...PICNICS, Etc.

Office and Stables,
WINCHESTER & OGDEN AVES. ... Chicago.

NELSON MORRIS. F. E. VOGEL. EDWARD MORRIS. HERBERT N. MORRIS.

NELSON MORRIS & CO.

Dressed Beef, Mutton and Pork

Lard Refiners, Supreme Brand Lard, Hams and Bacon.

FAIRBANK CANNING CO. PACKERS OF LION BRAND CANNED GOODS.

Union Stock Yards, Chicago, Ill. National Stock Yards, East St. Louis, Ill.

BOARD OF COUNTY COMMISSIONERS.

GUSTAV W. KUNSTMAN.

CHARLES BURMEISTER.

JOHN N. CUNNING.
Chairman Public Service Committee.

LOUIS H. MACK.

JAMES M. MUNN.

GUSTAV EHRHARDT, PRESIDENT. HENRY W. SCHLUETER, SECRETARY.

Congress Construction Co...

CARPENTERS and GENERAL CONTRACTORS

112-114 Dearborn Street

BOYCE BUILDING. Phone, Main 1499. Chicago

JAMES A. MILLER & BRO.

Slate
Tin
Tile and Iron

Roofers . .

Galvanized Iron and Copper
Cornices, Bays
Skylights, etc.

Special Attention . . . .
to Large First-Class Work
Fully Guaranteed

129-131 South Clinton St.
Chicago.

THOMAS CONNELLY
CHICAGO, ILL.

MANUFACTURER OF
STANDARD · · VITRIFIED · · SALT-GLAZED
SEWER PIPE
WALL COPING, FLUE LINING, DRAIN TILE, CEMENT, ETC., ETC.
OFFICE, 312-313 OXFORD BLUILDING, 84 LA SALLE STREET.
TELEPHONE MAIN 609

TELEPHONE MAIN 5368.

THE CARL ANDERSON CO.
GENERAL MACHINE SHOP

19 TO 23 S. JEFFERSON STREET,

Stationery and Marine Engines,
Boilers, Pumps and Well-Boring Machinery. · · · CHICAGO

REPAIRING AND JOBBING PROMPTLY ATTENDED TO.

BOARD OF COUNTY COMMISSIONERS.

DAVID MARTIN.

JOHN RITTER.

THOMAS J. McNICHOLS.
Chairman Building Committee.

JOHN A. LINN.

GEORGE D. UNOLD.

The Largest and Only Establishment in the World Devoted
Exclusively to the Manufacture of

Jail Cells and Iron Work for Prisons

The Pauly Jail Building & Manufacturing Company

Office, 2215 DeKalb Street ST. LOUIS, MO.

Hardened Steel Cells
Patent Rotary Cells
Common Iron Cells
Calaboose Cages

Steel and Iron Doors
Prison Window Guards
Iron Bunks
Jail Locks, Etc.

CORRESPONDENCE SOLICITED.

BOARD OF COUNTY COMMISSIONERS.

OSCAR D. ALLEN.

THEODORE W. JONES.

HENRY J. BEER.

GEORGE STRUCKMAN.

ESTABLISHED 1851

OLDEST GROCERY HOUSE IN CHICAGO.

Durand & Kasper Co.

Our New Building, Lake, Union and Eagle Sts., which we will occupy about May.

Wholesale Grocers Importers and Manufacturers....

19, 21, 23 & 25 MARKET STREET

ESTABLISHED 1857. INCORPORATED 1882.

W. M. HOYT COMPANY,

IMPORTERS AND MANUFACTURERS.

Wholesale Grocers

OFFICE AND WAREHOUSE:

1 to 11 Michigan Avenue, and 1 to 9 River Street.

FORT DEARBORN COFFEE AND SPICE MILLS AND MANUFACTORY:

6 & 8 River Street.

T. N. JAMIESON,
Superintendent of Public Service.

McNEIL & HIGGINS CO.

Wholesale Grocers and Importers

3, 5, 7, 9, 11 & 13 LAKE ST., COR. MICHIGAN AVE.

CHICAGO, ILL.

C. B. SHEFLER, President and Manager. N. C. FISHER, Secretary and Treasurer.

TELEPHONE MAIN 5102.

The Garden City Sand Co.

FIRE BRICK, WALL COPING, FLUE LINING, PORTLAND LOUISVILLE CEMENT, ACME CEMENT PLASTER, FIRE PROOFING, PARTITION TILE, SAND OF EVERY KIND, CRUSHED QUARTZ, ETC.

Suite 1010, Security Bldg, Fifth Ave. and Madison St., Chicago.

ESTABLISHED 1857.

Sprague, Smith & Co.

MERCHANTS, MANUFACTURERS, IMPORTERS.

Plate Glass, Window Glass of all Kinds, Picture Glass, Rough, Ribbed, Colored, Cathedral, Enameled and Chipped Glass, French and German Looking Glass Plates.

207 & 209 Randolph St., Chicago.

EOS THE WONDER OF THE AGE!

Eos does the Family Washing while you sleep.
Eos is Woman's Best Friend.

Eos is unique in its composition and action, and totally unapproached in value by any other preparation.

JAMES L. MONAGHAN,
Deputy County Comptroller.

Evans Marble Company

Importers, Producers, Manufacturers and Wholesale Dealers in

Italian and Tennessee Marbles For Building Interiors.

Plumbers' Slabs, Furniture Marble, Mantels and Monumental Stock.

Telephone Harrison 552.

225 Dearborn Street, Chicago
Rooms 405 and 406.

FRANK L. DAVIS, Manager.

Contractors for Marble and Mosaic Work on New Criminal Court Building and Cook County Jail Bldg.

Western Bank Note Company.

New Fire-Proof Building. CHICAGO.

Steel Plate and Lithographic Engraving and Printing.

BONDS

For Railways, Towns and Cities, Real Estate Bonds, Street Railways, Water Works, and Gas Companies.

Certificates of Stock, Drafts, Checks, Letter and Bill Headings, Etc., for Railways, Banks, Merchants and Corporations.

C. C. CHENEY, President.
C. A. CHAPMAN, Treasurer.
C. HEINEMAN, Secretary.

Bonds and other securelies engraved by this Company accepted on the New York Stock Exchange.

LOUIS LEWIN. SAMUEL LEVIN.
MAX BRO.

A. LEWIN & SON

Manufacturers of

Negligee Shirts, Pants and Overalls

187 & 189 Market Street,

CHICAGO.

ELECTRICAL SUPPLIES

FOR ALL PURPOSES.

Wholesale and Retail

Orders Carefully and Promptly Filled.

STORE AND WAREROOMS
173-175 ADAMS ST.

Central Electric Company

CHICAGO.

E. J. McCARTHY,
Chief Clerk Comptroller's Office.

LESLIE H. MILLER,
Chief Clerk Superintendent of Public Service Office.

Arc and Incandescent Light.
Electric Elevators.
Electric Power.

Wiring for all Branches of
Electric Service.
Electric Plants Installed.

Electrical Supplies.

CHICAGO EDISON COMPANY

EDISON BUILDING.

Telephone Main 1280. 139 Adams St., Chicago.

CHICAGO TELEPHONE COMPANY

GENERAL OFFICES:

203 Washington St., Chicago.

Operating Telephone Exchanges in Chicago and all Cities and Towns in the Counties of Cook, DuPage, Lake, McHenry, Kane, Kendall, Grundy and Will, in Illinois, and Lake and Porter in Indiana.

Estimates furnished for Speaking Tube, Private Line, Club Line and Telephone Exchange Service of every description.

ROBERT M. SIMON,
Chief Deputy County Clerk.

HENRY L. HERTZ,
Chief Deputy Clerk of the County Court.

PHILIP KNOPF,
County Clerk, County Comptroller, Clerk County Court,
Clerk Board of County Commissioners.

Into the Southland

AN ATTRACTIVE LINE

THE CHICAGO AND EASTERN ILLINOIS R·R·
TO FLORIDA AND THE SOUTH.

Chicago & Eastern Illinois R·R·

We shall appreciate the opportunity of sending you rates, maps and other information.

CHARLES L. STONE, General Passenger Agent, Chicago.
CITY TICKET OFFICE, 230 Clark Street.

ROBT. S. ILES,
County Attorney.

Up-To-Date Automatic... **Vacuum Method**

Used for correcting waters for boiler-feeding and utilizing waste steam for heating buildings is no experiment. Our apparatus and methods have clearly demonstrated their efficiency in maximum results and economy in all instances. No back pressure on engines while heating buildings or feedwater. Warm buildings and cleaner boilers guaranteed by Webster's improved vacuum system of Steam Heating and Vacuum Feed Water Heater and Purifier.

SEND FOR CATALOGUES....

WARREN, WEBSTER & COMPANY,

WORKS... CAMDEN, N. J.

Western Office, 1503-4 MONADNOCK BUILDING...CHICAGO.

WM. D. PICKELS, Manager.

TELEPHONE MAIN 3474.

John A. Donohue & Co.

..CEMENT PAVERS..

Office 43, 185 Dearborn Street,

CHICAGO.

Concrete Sidewalks,
Sidewalk Vault Covers,
Cellars and Driveways.

ESTIMATES MADE.

C. F. SAMMS. J. B. WANTZ.

Victor Electric Company

ELECTRICAL MANUFACTURERS AND CONTRACTORS

Dynamos and Motors Built and Repaired.
Experimental Work Done.

ESTIMATES GIVEN ON ALL KINDS OF ELECTRIC WORK.

218-220 E. Washington St.,
CHICAGO.

E. J. ZIMMER. E. M. SIMONDS.

E. J. ZIMMER & CO.

MANUFACTURERS OF

Paints and Varnish

RAILWAY, ROOFING AND ELASTIC CEMENT PAINTS, ETC.

Office: 266-8 Wabash Avenue,
TELEPHONE MAIN 4381.

ESTIMATES GIVEN ON ALL KINDS OF WORK.

CHICAGO.

FACTORY: VALPARAISO, IND.

BUY TELEPHONES THAT ARE GOOD. Not Cheap Things.

The difference in cost is little. We guarantee our apparatus and guarantee our customers against loss by patent suits. Our guarantee and instruments are both good.

Western Telephone Construction Co.

Largest Manufacturers of Telephones in the United States.

250-254 S. CLINTON STREET,
CHICAGO.

N. W. TAYLOR. GEO. H. TAYLOR. JAMES T. MIX.

GEO. H. TAYLOR & CO.

WHOLESALE **PAPER** DEALERS

We carry a Complete Line of the Following:
Bond, Ledger, and All Grades Flat Writing Papers, Cardboards, Book and Cover Papers, Etc. Tileston & Hollingsworth's Plate and Other Grades.
A SPECIALTY OF PRINTING PAPER IN ROLLS.

207 & 209 Monroe Street,

CHICAGO.

WARREN H. MILNER,
County Architect.

HENRY SCHERER, Pres't. D. HALLE, Vice-Pres't. JOHN T. SWARTHOUT, Sec'y.

The Henry Scherer Manufacturing Co.

Manufacturers of and Dealers in

Sash, Doors and Blinds, Mouldings, Window Frames, Brackets, Balusters, Stair Work, Etc.

Telephone Main 4509. 416-426 Blue Island Avenue, Chicago.

W. S. EDWARDS MFG. CO.

MAKERS OF FINE

Gas and Electric Light Fixtures

21 EAST LAKE STREET,

BETWEEN WABASH AND MICHIGAN AVES.

Telephone Main 329. CHICAGO.

OFFICIALS OF COOK COUNTY AGENT'S OFFICE.

CHARLES F. PASDELOUP,
Assistant County Agent.

MEYER COSSMAN,
Secretary County Agent.

GEO. S. OLESON,
County Agent.

W. P. GUNTHORP, PRES'T.
PERCY GUNTHORP, VICE-PRES'T.
J. LATHAM WARREN, SEC'Y

TELEPHONE MAIN 1920.

... THE ...

GUNTHORP-WARREN PRINTING CO...

LAW PRINTERS ..

NOS. 51, 53, 55
DEARBORN STREET,

CHICAGO

...THE....

WM. SCHMIDT BAKING CO.

Telephone North 241.

Crackers
... and Fine Biscuits

75-81 CLYBOURN AVE.,
CHICAGO.

ESTABLISHED 1862.

CHAS. ZSCHUPPE
LOCKSMITH

SAFES OPENED AND REPAIRED.

ELECTRIC AND MECHANICAL BELL HANGING, SPEAKING TUBES INSERTED AND ALL KINDS OF IRON WORK MADE AND REPAIRED.

168 MICHIGAN ST., — — CHICAGO.
OPPOSITE COUNTY CRIMINAL COURT BUILDING.

JOHN P. FOWLER,

Spring Beds, Mattresses, Cots

IRON BEDS, FEATHERS,
COMFORTERS, ETC.

1434 Wabash Ave., Chicago.

Hospital Furnishings a Specialty. Tel. South 637.

JOHN C. SPRY, Pres't. S. A. SPRY, Vice-Pres't.
GEO. E. SPRY, Sec'y and Treas.

JOHN SPRY LUMBER CO.

WHOLESALE
LUMBER...

Ashland Ave., South of 22d Street

TELEPHONES { Canal 32. " 46. CHICAGO.

WM. SULLIVAN

STEAM, HOT WATER AND HOT AIR
..HEATING APPARATUS..

VENTILATING

179 ILLINOIS STREET, CHICAGO
ESTIMATES FURNISHED.
PHONE NORTH 849.

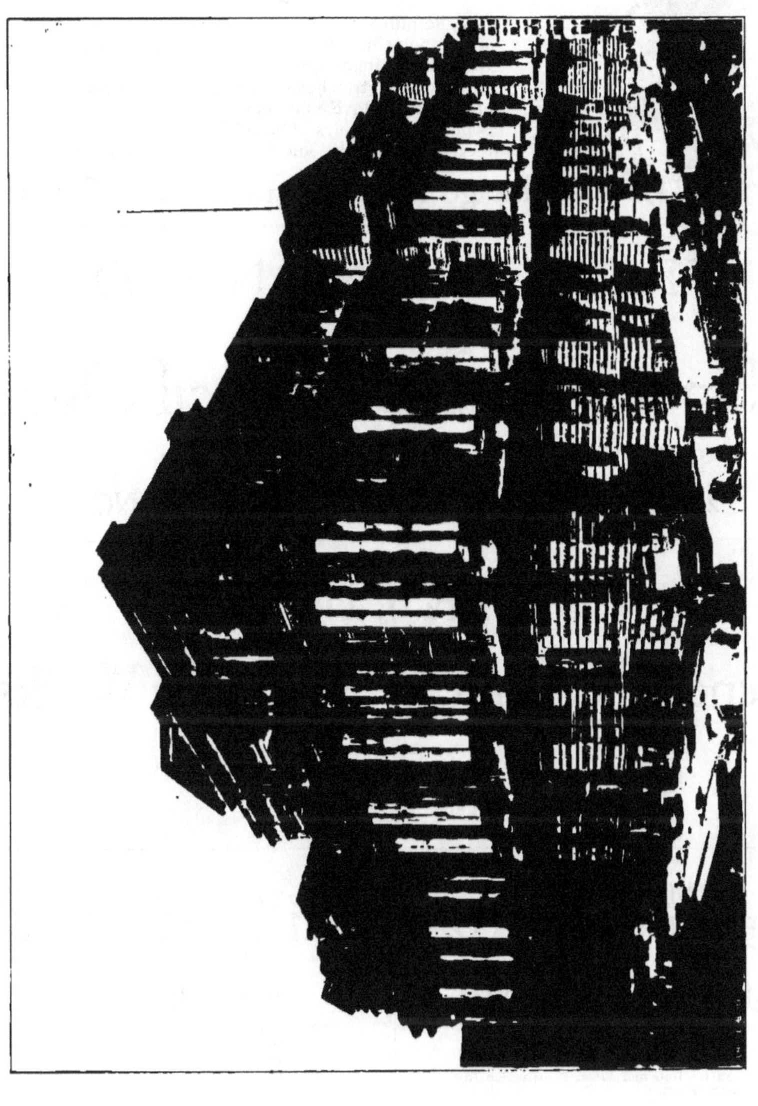

COOK COUNTY COURT HOUSE.

Make Your Face Known

Get the public familiar with your looks—that's a strong point in advertising. We can give you an elegant half-tone engraving of yourself which can be used on letter heads, cards, etc., for a couple of dollars. Have you seen some of our work? Send for our samples. Our colored calendar sent on receipt of 10c—the finest "Poster" calendar out.

Chicago Photo Engraving Co., Chicago

FRANK T. SCANLAN & CO.

Sole Agents and Dealers in the Famous

Shipping Clerks' Council Cigar

Also Choice Brands of Imported and Domestic Liquors.

226 LA SALLE STREET, CORNER QUINCY

JOSEPH J. DUFFY

General Contractor for Public Works

161 LA SALLE STREET, CHICAGO

TELEPHONE MAIN 4588.

MACKOLITE FIRE PROOFING CO.

MANUFACTURERS AND CONTRACTORS OF

Light Fire Proofing Material

Partition Tile, Plaster Boards, Deafening Material, Fire Proof Lathing, Furring Tile, General Fire Proofing, Fire Proof Protection for Iron and Wood Construction in Every Form.

FACTORY, CHICAGO HEIGHTS, ILL.

OFFICE: ROOM 1303 SCHILLER BUILDING

103-109 RANDOLPH STREET, CHICAGO.

Philip Henrici

Fancy Bakery
Delicacies and
Restaurant

108 & 110 EAST RANDOLPH STREET
CHICAGO

COOK COUNTY CRIMINAL COURT BUILDING.

AUG. ZANDER, Pres't and Treas.
Residence, 239 Bissell Street.

OSCAR A. REUM, Secretary.
Residence, 260 Racine Ave.

WILLIAM ZANDER, Gen'l Supt.
Box 380, Builders' and Traders' Exchange

AUG. ZANDER COMPANY,

CONTRACTORS FOR

Plain and Ornamental Plastering

ALL GRADES OF METAL AND WIRE LATHING
AND "SOLID PLASTER" PARTITIONS.

Room 40, Lakeside Building, S. W. Cor. Clark and Adams Sts.

Telephone Main Express 331. CHICAGO.

CONTRACTORS OF THE FOLLOWING REPRESENTATIVE BUILDINGS:

Cook County Jail, Asylum for Insane at Anna, Ill., St. Elizabeth Hospital, Stock Exchange Building, Hartford Building, Siegel, Cooper & Co. Stores, Haymarket and Windsor Theatres, Residences of A. O. Slaughter, F. J. Dewes, Conrad Seipp, and the Haskell Museum of the Chicago University.

Telephone Main 819. ESTABLISHED 1868.

Nowak Construction Co.

MANUFACTURERS OF

Turnbull & Cullerton

STEEL, LATH AND
MONARCH FIRE PROOFING,

195 LaSalle Street, Chicago.

Send for Sample and Catalogue.

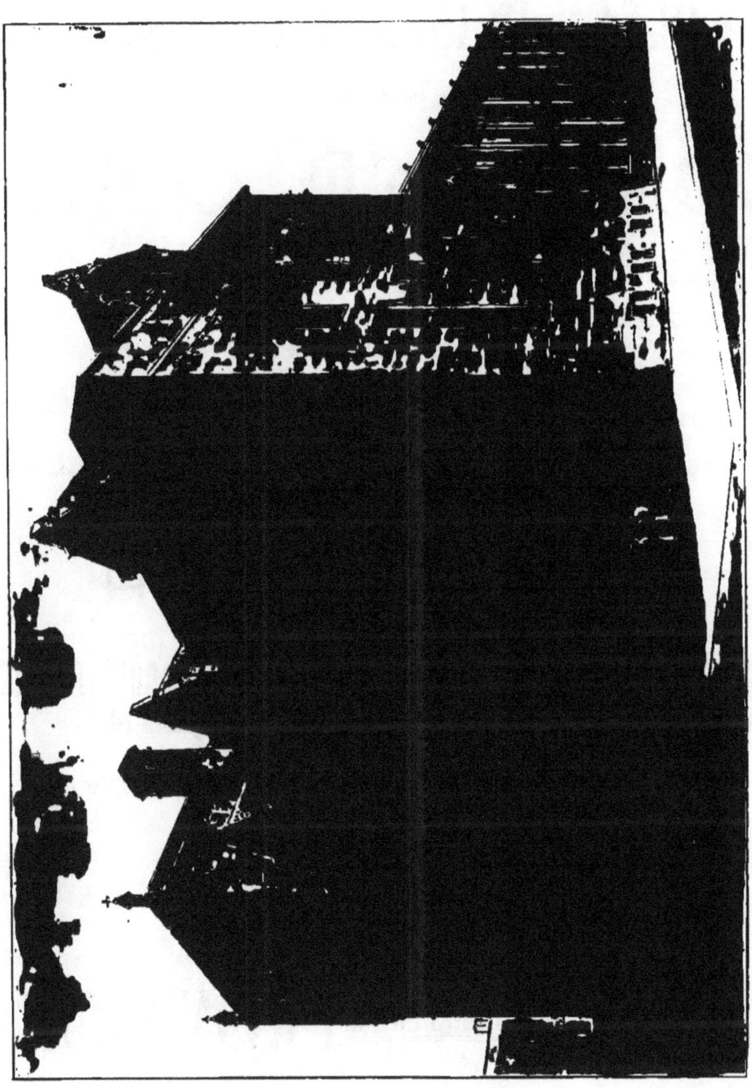

NEW COOK COUNTY JAIL.

G. GOLSEN. G. B. HEISEN.

GOLSEN, HEISEN & COMPANY,

MINERS AND SHIPPERS OF

COAL AND COKE

MAIN OFFICE:

225 DEARBORN STREET.

TELEPHONE HARRISON 21.

RAIL YARDS: 505 SOUTH CLARK STREET.
TELEPHONE MAIN 72.
3129-3131 SOUTH CANAL STREET.
TELEPHONE SOUTH 719.

CHICAGO, ILL.

SHARP & SMITH,

MANUFACTURERS OF

THE CELEBRATED RANDOLPH COVERED ELASTIC ABDOMINAL SUPPORTERS AND BANDAGES.

ARTIFICIAL LIMBS AND EYES.

73 Randolph Street, Chicago.

ARMOUR & CO.

PACKERS AND DEALERS IN PROVISIONS

205 LaSALLE STREET,

CHICAGO.

COOK COUNTY HOSPITAL, EAST END.
James H. Graham, Warden.

ESTABLISHED 1886

AMERICAN EXCHANGE NATIONAL BANK

...CHICAGO.

CAPITAL, $1,000,000.

SURPLUS, $225,000.

OFFICERS:

ROBERT STUART, - President.
W. C. SEIPP, - - Vice-President.
ROBERT M. ORR, - Cashier.
ARTHUR TOWER, - Asst. Cashier
J. EDW. MAASS, - 2d Asst. Cashier.

DIRECTORS:

ROBERT STUART.
W. C. SEIPP.
D. K. PEARSONS.
L. C. HUCK.
E. W. GILLETT.
J. A. MARKLEY.
I. K. HAMILTON.
J. C. WELLING.
W. H. SWIFT.
CLARENCE BUCKINGHAM.
THOMAS E. WELLS.

COOK COUNTY HOSPITAL—Western End. M. R. MANDELBAUM, Chief Clerk.

WILDMAN BROS.

THE EXPERT

BOILER MANUFACTURERS AND REPAIRERS.

87 TO 93

NORTH CLINTON ST.

...CHICAGO...

WHEN IN DOUBT

ORDER

FRIEDMAN'S

"BEST QUALITY"

OLEOMARGARINE

NONE BETTER.

Ornamental Boiler Fronts, Machinery and General Castings.

43 to 61 Indiana St., Chicago, Ill.

Bramhall, Deane & Co.

Duparquet, Huot & Moneuse Co.

OF CHICAGO

INCORPORATED

Deane, Huot, Brooks & Moneuse Co.

MANUFACTURERS OF

French Ranges and Cooking Apparatus

FOR HOTELS AND PUBLIC INSTITUTIONS.

79, 81 & 83 Market St., Chicago, Ill.

J. HUMPHREY, Pres't. H. HEMINGWAY, Sec'y and Treas.

TELEPHONE MAIN 1984.

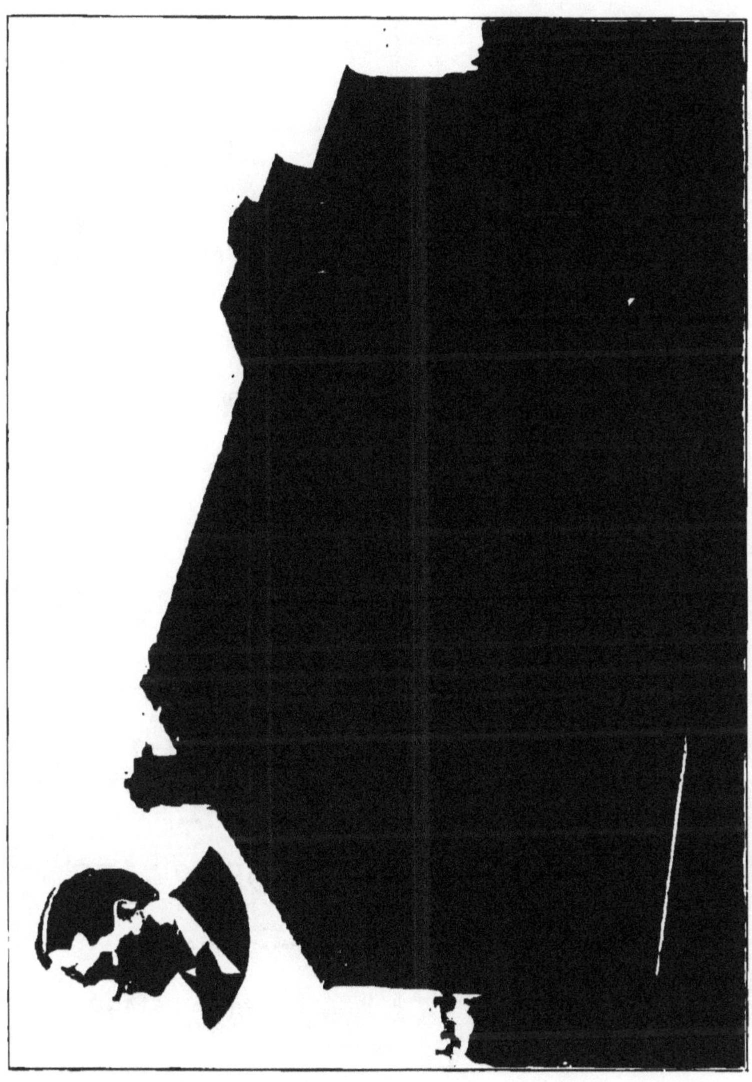

DETENTION HOSPITAL.
Dr. E. C. Fortner, County Physician.

LOVEDAY & VON DER HEIDE

PHOTOGRAPHERS

SCHILLER THEATER,

CHICAGO.

THE PHOTOGRAPHIC WORK OF THIS PUBLICATION WAS EXECUTED BY US.

KATZ, WEIL & MAY

IMPORTERS AND WHOLESALE DEALERS IN

...PURE...

WINES AND LIQUORS

64 SHERMAN STREET,

CHICAGO.

THE MILLER

CHEMICAL

Fire

Extinguisher

In use and adopted as the standard machine by the leading corporations and business firms throughout the country.

The Miller Fire Pail

Patent, Automatic Cover. Dust Proof. No Evaporation. No Odor. Simplest and best Fire Pail ever patented. Thousands in use.

MILLER CHEMICAL ENGINE CO.

13 North State Street,

CHICAGO.

A. MUNCH

CONTRACTOR FOR ALL KINDS OF

CEMENT FLOORS

AND

SIDE WALKS

BOX 378 BUILDERS & TRADERS EXCHANGE,

144 CLEVELAND AVE.,

CHICAGO, ILL.

ALL MY WORK IS GUARANTEED FOR TEN YEARS.
ESTIMATES FURNISHED ON APPLICATION.
PUBLIC WORK A SPECIALTY.

COOK COUNTY MORGUE. J. E. McNICHOLS, Asst. Chief Clerk.

W. S. BOGLE, President. T. A. BROUGHTON, Vice-President and Gen'l Manager.

...THE...

Crescent Coal and Mining Co.

PRODUCERS OF

ANTHRACITE **COAL** BITUMINOUS

General Offices, Rookery Building,

CHICAGO.

WORTHINGTON STEAM PUMPS

THE STANDARD FOR ALL DUTIES.

Boiler Feed Pumps, Brewery Pumps, Fire Pumps, Low Steam Pressure Pumps, Water Works Pumping Engines. Water Meters for Hot or Cold Water, Meters for Crude Oil, Naphtha, Etc.

HENRY R. WORTHINGTON.

Chicago, 187-9 Van Buren St., Boston, 70 Kilby St., New York, 86 & 88 Liberty St., Philadelphia, 724 Arch St., St. Louis, 8th and St. Charles St., Cleveland, 24 South Water St., Detroit, 155 Jefferson Ave., Indianapolis, 64 South Pennsylvania St.

HENRY R. WORTHINGTON,

By JOHN CAREY.

VIEW OF COOK COUNTY POOR HOUSE.
Geo. F Morgan, Superintendent.

ANNUAL REPORT OF HON. DANIEL D. HEALY

President Board of County Commissioners of Cook County.

In presenting the exhaustive audible report of President Healy, it seems essentially germane to the subject to refer in congratulatory terms to the admirable condition to which the affairs of the county have been brought during the administration of President Healy.

The executive ability displayed in producing such commendable results indicate a genius for improvement such as is possessed by few men in so large a degree as has been shown by Mr. Healy. His methods have been so thorough in their completeness that their conception and execution stamp him as an indubitable master in administrative ability. The high order of excellence to which the diverse affairs of the county have been brought at the minimum of expense is in a large measure due to the wise direction of the present honored President of the County Board, and the President is consequently deservedly one of the most praiseworthy heads of the County Board that Cook County has ever had. It would be a work of mere supererogation to extol his efficiency and conscientious fidelity to the interests committed to his zealous care. Among those who have kept themselves informed of his plans and achievements for the betterment of the affairs of Cook County, they—and their name is legion—regard him as a decidedly unique President, admirably adapted for the office which he has so signally dignified during his incumbency of it.

THE REPORT—IT SPEAKS FOR ITSELF.

At the beginning of the year I submitted a statement showing the resources and liabilities of the County, and such other information as seemed to me to be for the best interests of the County. I feel gratified that my recommendations during the past year have been so well received and, generally, favorably acted upon.

THE COUNTY COURT HOUSE.

The congested condition of all the offices in the Court House, the increase in the volume of business of the County in all its branches is proof conclusive of the great need of more room in this building in order to properly accommodate the public business. Careful consideration has been given to the suggestion to build two additional stories to the present structure and thus secure the needed room.

CITY AN ILLEGAL OCCUPANT.

This was finally deemed inadvisable at this time, in view of the fact that legal proceedings are now pending in the courts against the City of Chicago, as to its illegal occupancy with a building for city purposes of the west half of block 39, original town of Chicago, the title to which rests in Cook County. Pending a decision of the case the imperative demand for additional court room has been met by renting in the Chicago Opera House such rooms as were necessary for holding courts.

SANITARY IMPROVEMENTS.

During the past year the entire sanitary condition of the Court House has been overhauled, and all old plumbing torn out and the system changed and replaced with the latest improved sanitary fixtures. Owing to the massive construction of the building, the securing of proper ventilation and light has proven a knotty problem. This has, however, been solved during the past year ; the whole

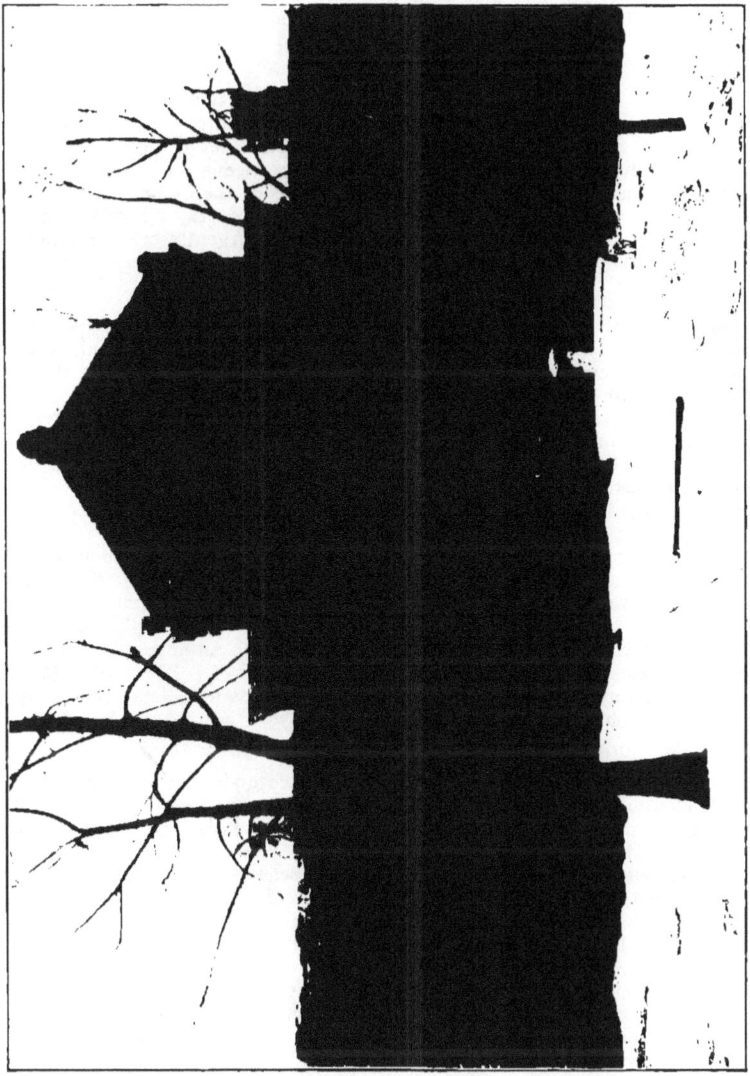

ADMINISTRATION BUILDING, COOK COUNTY INSANE ASYLUM.

plan of ventilation has been changed, and a new system of pipes, flues and ventilators through the walls into all rooms has been put in, which is now in successful operation.

Electric lights have been placed in the halls, which, with the introduction of pure air and light and the improved sanitary condition, all that could be reasonably expected has been accomplished.

THE COUNTY HOSPITAL.

This institution has been taxed to its fullest capacity during the past year, owing to the natural increase growing out of an increased population and a large number of people attracted here expecting to find employment at high and remunerative wages, failing and disappointed, and without friends and means, through want and exposure, fell sick and thus found refuge in the County Hospital and became a charge upon the County. These conditions necessitated increased appropriations both for the Hospital, Poor House and County Agent's outdoor relief. I do not now see that these conditions will change or decrease during the coming year.

ADDITIONAL FACILITIES.

Protection to the public, as well as humanity to the afflicted from contagious diseases, proves the wisdom of the timely action in the erection and equipment of the new Hospital Pavilion addition to the County Hospital, set apart for the care and treatment of contagious diseases.

The new Detention Hospital is admirably adapted to the purpose intended. The accommodations for the insane and dependent children pending their weekly examinations by the Court, which are held in the building, are ample and fitted with modern conveniences. The consolidation of the Detention Hospital with the County Hospital, under the management of the Warden of the Hospital, has resulted in greater efficiency, better discipline and a reducing of expenses.

The electric equipment has been made efficient by removing all old mains and wires from the tunnel and replacing them with new mains and wires; the grounds are lighted with arc lights; the passenger elevators in the Administration Building and the freight elevators in the east and west corridors of the Hospital have been overhauled and thoroughly repaired; the interior of the Administration Building has been painted and decorated, and the stairways repaired. The entire Hospital plant has been improved by such repairs throughout as were found necessary to keep the institution in first-class condition.

HOSPITAL LABORATORY—A GREAT DESIDERATUM.

In accordance with the report of your Committee under date of March 25, the Superintendent of Public Service was instructed to fit up a Clinic Laboratory at the County Hospital for scientific and experimental purposes, the cost and maintenance of the same to be paid from the funds received by the Warden from the sale of clinic tickets, donations, etc., and providing that no expense be incurred without first being authorized by the Board. The establishment of this branch of medicine in the Hospital was urgently advocated by the Hospital Medical Staff as essential and necessary and in line with the advancement of medical science in the treatment of diseases by microscopical examination of bacteria of diseases and the manufacture of serum for treatment of tuberculosis, erysipelas, etc., and the manufacture of antitoxin for diphtheria and other contagious diseases, as well as keeping and preserving specimens for information of the House Physicians and Medical Staff. It is hoped that the Cook County Clinic Laboratory will prove beneficial.

COUNTY MANUFACTURING OF DRUGS.

During the year, by advice of your Committee, you have now in successful operation, under the direction of a competent pharmacist, a department for the

END VIEW COOK COUNTY INSANE ASYLUM.

manufacture of drugs and chemicals. This departure from the original method of purchasing outright in the market all drugs required in the Hospital is now an assured success, not only from an economical standpoint, but insures a higher grade and a purer quality of drugs at less expense.

MERITED COMMENDATION.

Warden Graham's business management has proven him to be a patient and efficient officer.

The County Morgue was planned and constructed to accommodate the needs of the County and City for years to come. It is the largest and best adapted building of its kind in this country.

CARE OF THE INSANE.

The Board has, by placing the Insane Asylum and Poor House under the management of a General Superintendent, charged with the conduct of its business affairs and the discipline of its employes, done much to maintain the deservedly high standard in which it stands as compared with other similar institutions.

The control and treatment of patients in this institution is now, for the first time, under the sole management of an able corps of physicians, appointed by reason of their fitness to treat this class of cases; and this has resulted in a largely increased percentage of cures. This is especially gratifying when we take into consideration the fact that the only class of cases the State Institutions will receive from the County are those whose maladies show some evidence of yielding to treatment and ultimate recovery.

In the selection of attendants to care for the unfortunate charges, intelligence and humanity have been considered as the first qualifications for those positions, and great care has been exercised in each case in their selection.

COMPETENT MEDICAL STAFF.

The Committee appointed, under the resolution of Commissioner Allen to recommend a Supervising Medical Staff, to have charge of the medical treatment and care of the patients in the County Insane Asylum, submitted to the Board resolutions as their report, under date of September 23, 1895, and recommended Dr. Richard Dewey, Dr. Sanger Brown and Dr. Archibald Church be selected as the Supervising Medical Staff. I would recommend that Dr. D. W. Lewis and Dr. Wm. Cuthbertson be selected to serve as said Supervising Medical Staff for the term expiring on the first Monday of October, 1896. This Medical Staff has been authorized to make rules and regulations governing the resident physicians, nurses and attendants, and the care and treatment of the patients; such rules and regulations to be approved by this Board before becoming operative. They are empowered to inspect and inquire into the condition of the Institution and the medical treatment of the inmates.

The gentlemen I have above suggested to act as the Medical Staff are recognized by the medical profession as eminent authority in the treatment of this particular class of diseases. From this Staff this Board may reasonably hope to receive valuable suggestions and recommendations. By frequent visits to the Institution their presence alone will exert an excellent influence, and I confidently predict good results from their supervision.

VARIOUS REPAIRS, ETC.

During the year nine old boilers have been taken out and replaced with nine new boilers, with fittings complete, and such repairs made to the heating apparatus as to insure comfort.

A new fire pump has been added to the machinery equipment, and the necessary hose provided for fire protection.

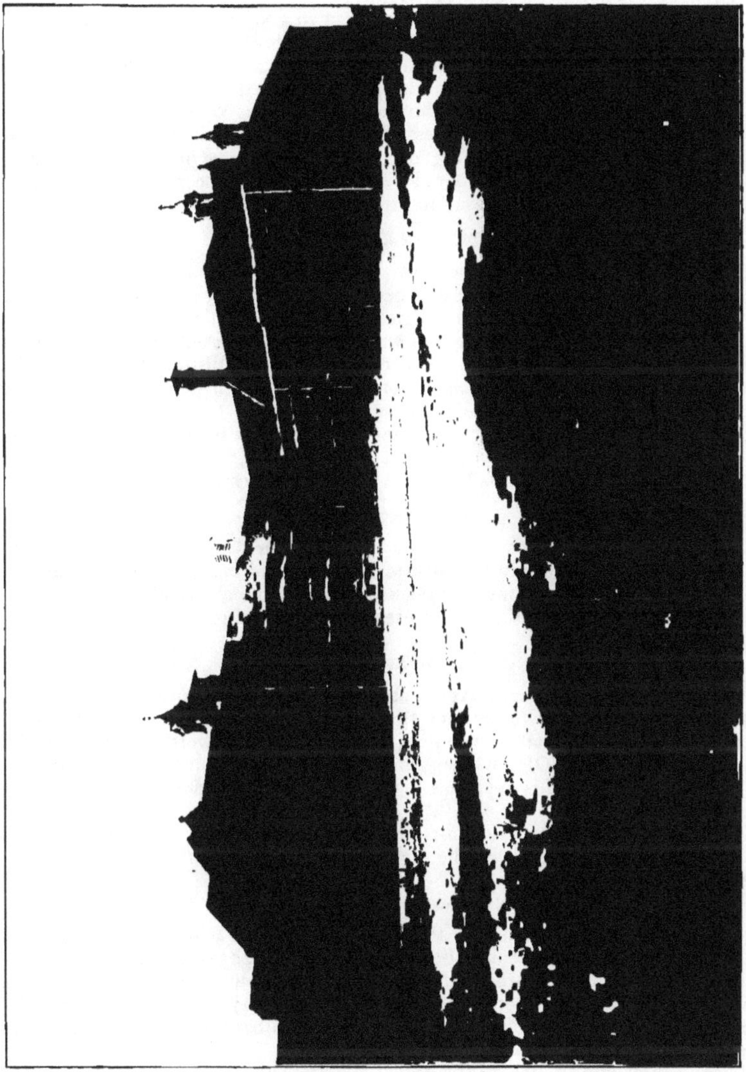

DETACHED WARD, COOK COUNTY INSANE ASYLUM.

An ample supply of water is now assured by the laying of an 8-inch main from the City main supply pipe at Irving Park to and in the grounds of the institution. Fire plugs and connections have been placed in the grounds and buildings at convenient points in case of emergency.

The buildings have been improved and kept in good repair, and by placing the receipts and disbursements of all supplies and the control of the employes under the direct supervision of a business manager, many abuses have been corrected, economy secured, and the service and discipline improved.

The excellent condition of the Dunning institutions reflects credit upon General Superintendent Morgan's business management and his able assistants, Drs. McGrew, Johnson, Kearney and Ferguson, of the Insane Asylum, and Drs. Crowe, Ospray and Crowely, of the Poor House. Chief Engineer Quinn has given valuable service and has made many improvements in his department.

THE POOR HOUSE.

This institution is one of the most difficult of proper management. Many persons who have no right to be charges upon the County seek this asylum as a home for the winter. Such as are physically able to perform manual labor are given suitable tasks in the building and watching the premises. Such employment, however, is limited to the necessary requirements of the institution from day to day, and can only be regarded as a means of something for idle hands to do. As a large number of the inmates are apparently incapable to attend to their own wants, such persons require more than ordinary skill and experience to manage without trouble. The bad element, always present in such an institution, is eliminated as soon as possible, it being the only means by which deserving cases can be cared for.

THE COUNTY FARM.

During the present year the County Farm has yielded a large amount of supplies for the use of the Dunning institutions. The land is increasing in value, and its products fully pay the County for the amount invested at market prices.

It furnished supplies during the present year, at market prices, to the value of $5,776.47.

CREDIT DULY ACCORDED.

The duties of the County Agent are exacting, and require the most careful attention and watchfulness to see that the large amount of money is honestly and properly expended, and that it only goes to those who are worthy and entitled to relief. Agent George F. Oleson deserves the highest credit for the able manner in which he has conducted this department, as also does his efficient assistant, Charles Pasdeloup.

It seems to me one of the most difficult problems this Board has to contend with is the proper expenditure of the money appropriated for the care and relief of the poor.

INTERESTING STATISTICS.

In the appropriation for the present year there was set aside for the supplies for the County Agent's Department, $100,000; for salaries, $25,000. These sums will be entirely used, and are hardly sufficient to meet the most urgent calls upon this department. In addition, there was appropriated $14,275 for out-door relief in the country towns. These figures show that this Board will pay out this year $140,000 in caring for the needy poor.

These figures do not include the cost of keeping the paupers at the Poor House. It is a fact, established by the records at the County Agent's office, that the greater share of this money is used during the six months commencing October 1 and ending March 31. The same is true in regard to the increased numbers who have

BOARD OF COOK COUNTY CIVIL SERVICE COMMISSIONERS.

SAMUEL M. BURDETT.

EDWARD D. NORTHAM. JAMES D. MORRISON.

to be provided for at the Poor House. This condition exists largely from the fact that so many men willing to work cannot find employment during the winter months, and are not able to earn wages high enough during the summer to carry them and their families through a severe winter.

The County Agent's report for October shows that the total number of families aided was 1,477. Of this number 592 were married men, 15 widowers and 2 single men. The Poor House report shows a daily average of about 800 men.

October being the first month when real needs of the poor commence to demand attention, the figures of this month are not near so large as the other months, when it becomes colder and their needs greater.

SOME PERTINENT SUGGESTIONS.

These figures will show that during October Cook County wholly or in part supported in round numbers between 1,400 and 1,500 men. The coming five months the number will be larger, probably increased at least 50 per cent. For this large amount of money so expended Cook County receives nothing in return.

It has occurred to me that some plan might be devised whereby Cook County might receive some value for this amount of money. Taking these figures, it would seem only fair to say that during the winter months the County has 500 able-bodied men who could earn their living if a way was provided for them to do so.

Could not these men be put to work on the streets keeping them free from snow and mud in connection with the City street cleaning department, the County to pay them a small sum, equivalent to what it now costs to care for them?

Would not the City authorities co-operate with this Board in some manner whereby the men able to work, who are supported by Cook County, should render some service for what they receive?

Would not the men asking charity be more willing to avail themselves of some such arrangement rather than be classed as paupers?

I submit the matter to your careful consideration.

COUNTY ATTORNEY.

The County Attorney has from time to time reported to this Board the status and condition of all litigation now pending in the various courts in which Cook County is interested. Mr. Iles is entitled to great credit for the skill and energy which he has shown in the conduct of the Legal Department of the County.

Assistant County Attorney William F. Struckman has charge of that branch of the County Attorney's office pertaining to insane cases and dependent children brought before the County Court. In the discharge of this trust he has given faithful attention to public interests.

COUNTY PHYSICIAN.

The County Physician has charge of the insane committed to the Detention Hospital pending their examination and disposal by the County Court, as well as the care and welfare of dependent children coming through the County Agent's office. To these duties are added the medical attention and treatment of the prisoners in the County Jail. To Dr. Fortner I cheerfully accord praise for the efficient manner in which he has discharged these duties.

COOK COUNTY NORMAL SCHOOL.

The Cook County Normal School grounds consist of 17.12 acres described as the west half of the southeast quarter of Sec. 21, T. 38, N. R. 14 E. of the 3d P. M. Ten acres of this property was deeded by L. W. Beck and wife for Normal School purposes, April 24, 1860. The County has the abstract of title, continued to March 28, 1892. The maintenance of the Normal School amounts to an average cost of

FRANK J. GAULTER,
Clerk Circuit Court.

$36,000 per year. The Normal School is a problem which this Board should solve. I would recommend that the buildings and a portion of the grounds be turned over to the City Board of Education with the understanding that they maintain a normal school for the education of teachers for our public schools. The balance of this property should be subdivided and disposed of, the money to be used for building purposes. I have no doubt but that from $150,000 to $200,000 would be received from the sale of this property, and in the meantime relieve the County from the expense of maintaining said school.

THE OLD JAIL BUILDING.

The Old Jail Building has been for years a just cause of complaint and criticism. The law regards innocent all prisoners committed to the jail, until properly tried and convicted, as provided by law. It is just that in the interim between commitment and trial the prisoners should be treated with humanity and their health preserved. In order to secure this the new wing of the County Jail has been erected at a cost of about $100,000. It is estimated that it will require an additional outlay of $50,000 or $60,000 to furnish the cells and complete the new structure. This expense must be provided for in the next annual appropriation bill. The County will then have a jail fully equal to the real demands of justice.

THE NEW CRIMINAL COURT BUILDING.

During the past year this building has been completed by such changes in the arrangement of offices and court rooms as tended to facilitate the dispatch of public business. Furniture, where needed, has been provided, and the building in all its details is now equipped with modern appliances, and is a credit to the County and a model of convenience.

THE COUNTY JUDICIARY.

I believe the time has come when this Board and the people of this County should take the necessary steps towards urging the next General Assembly to amend the law in relation to the Criminal Court of Cook County. I think the present system whereby the Circuit and Superior Judges serve in the Criminal Court through a system of rotation should be abolished and three Judges selected whose sole duty should be confined to the Criminal Court. A Judge who is presiding in the Circuit or Superior Court and compelled to break off and go to the Criminal Court for three months, necessarily has more or less business pertaining to the Circuit or Superior Court to which he has to give some time while presiding at the Criminal Court; and his calendar stands still while he is in the Criminal Court. The present system is a source of delay to the common law and chancery litigants, and to the prompt trial of criminal cases. It is a source of expense to the County by reason of increased amount of jurors' salaries and cost of dieting prisoners whose cases are delayed, and in many other ways.

By having Judges who devote their entire time to the trial of criminal cases they would be able to dispatch a much greater volume of business in a term than is done under the present system, and the Circuit and Superior Court Judges would be able to give their entire time to the duties of their own Courts, which would work to the great advantage of the County and persons having business in the Courts.

In this connection I think it would be well to consider the question of an additional Judge for the County Court, or devise some method to relieve the County Court from its present condition.

CIVIL SERVICE COMMISSION.

The law creating the Cook County Civil Service Commission became operative July 1, and in accordance with its provisions I appointed three commissioners and reported my action to this Board at the time.

E. J. MAGERSTADT,
Clerk Criminal Court.

APPLICATIONS FOR POSITIONS.

During the five months of its existence the Commission has received over 1,500 applications for positions and has examined over 1,200 of the applicants. All the present employes of the County coming under the jurisdiction of this Board, and hence under the jurisdiction of the Civil Service Commission are on the classified list, and the benefits and advantages of civil service as applied to our employes are fast making themselves felt and the ultimate success of civil service is assured. The Commissioners have given careful attention to the study of the Act, and have been earnest in their efforts to administer the law according to its terms and provisions and in a practical, business-like manner.

NURSES AT COUNTY HOSPITAL.

In this connection I deem it my duty to call your attention to the question of nurses at the County Hospital. As you know, during this year they have been furnished by a contract with the Illinois Training School for Nurses at a cost of $22,200 for the year. In addition to this they have had the services of quite a number of convalescent patients who were able to leave the hospital but were retained there, assisting the nurses. At times the County has been called upon to bear the cost of feeding and caring for as high as from thirty to forty of this class.

This contract expires on the 31st day of this month and some different arrangement will have to be made for the coming year. Under the opinion of the County Attorney, dated September 17, the nurses and the medical staff at the Hospital will necessarily have to be appointed under the Act relating to the Civil Service Commission, and will be under the jurisdiction of that Board. I think it a question to be well considered whether the County cannot establish a Training School for nurses at the Hospital, whereby as high or higher standard may be obtained as can be had under a contract with a private school.

At present under the system in vogue the same nurses only stay a few months as a rule, and are then sent to other charges more profitable to the school. By this method the County Hospital, as to a large per cent of the nurses, is simply a primary or kindergarten department. Nurses appointed after a competitive examination and retaining their positions as long as they performed their duty and receiving a proper compensation, in my judgment, would render better service than those now there without compensation simply for the necessary experience to fit them for other positions. As to the Hospital Staff and this question of nurses I would recommend either the Hospital Committee or a special Committee at once take the matter up and submit a plan to this Board for its approval before the consideration of the appropriation bill.

A SEASONABLE EULOGY.

The office of the Superintendent of Public Service deserves more than a passing notice. This department is charged with the expenditure of nearly three-quarters of a million dollars annually, and I challenge any person to make a just criticism of the manner in which this office is conducted, or to deny the statement that every cent of the County's money paid out is only paid out for full value received. The aim of the Superintendent and his able assistant has been to encourage all the honest competition possible, and it cannot be said that any clique or ring of merchants, salesmen or contractors have any inside influence in the matter of furnishing Cook County with supplies. In this office none but business methods prevail, and depending, as this Board has to do, upon the Superintendent to so great an extent for the proper expenditure of so large a sum of money, it is most gratifying to me, and it must be to the members of this Board, to have the office filled by so capable and efficient an officer as Dr. T. N. Jamieson.

ABIJAH O. COOPER,
Clerk Probate Court.

INDUSTRIAL SCHOOLS.

The Industrial School trouble has lately been so thoroughly aired that you are all conversant with all questions pertaining to the relation of this County to the various Industrial Schools. I only suggest that before appropriating any sum to them next year a careful investigation be made, and proper restrictions thrown around such appropriations as will insure their expenditure for the purpose for which this Board intends them.

RESOURCES OF COOK COUNTY.

From the certificate of the County Clerk the equalized valuation of all classes of property in Cook County for the year 1895 is as follows:

Real estate	$213,029,549
Personal property	38,531,171
Railroad property	19,183,816
Total	$270,745,536

To maintain the County Government, including the payment of principal and interest of the bonded debt incurred by the County since August 8, 1870, for the year 1896, the County is allowed by law to levy as a tax an amount equal to 75 cents on the $100 equalized valuation of all taxable property for the year 1895, being the last previous assessment, which amount will be $2,030,584.02 for the year 1896.

ESTIMATED RECEIPTS FOR 1896.

The estimated receipts of County Offices in and for the year 1896 over and above the salaries legally to be paid out of said receipts will be about as follows:

County Treasurer and ex-officio County Collector	$ 310,000 00
Recorder of Deeds	190,000 00
County Clerk and Clerk of County Court	200,000 00
Clerk of Probate Court	100,000 00
Clerk of Circuit Court	180,000 00
Clerk of Superior Court	120,000 00
Sheriff	50,000 00
Clerk of Criminal Court	2,000 00
Coroner	1,000 00
Total	$1,153,000 00
Available resources will be from tax levy	2,030,584 02
Add estimated receipts from County Offices	1,153,000 00
Making total from all sources	$3,183,584 02

The fixed charges are the principal on bonded indebtedness incurred since August 8, 1870.

BONDED INDEBTEDNESS.

OLD INDEBTEDNESS.

May 1, 1880, 4½ per cent Refunding bonds, Series A, expire May 1, 1900	$1,158,500 00
May 1, 1885, 4 per cent Refunding bonds, series B, expire May 1, 1905	500,000 00
Total	$1,658,500 00

NEW INDEBTEDNESS.

May 1, 1888, 4 per cent Refunding bonds, expire $50,000 each year	$ 650,000 00
February 1, 1889, 5 per cent Court House bonds, expire January 1, 1899	750,000 00
May 1, 1892, 1 to 20 years 4 per cent Refunding bonds, Series C, expire $67,500 each year	1,147,500 00
Total	$2,547,500 00

RECAPITULATION.

Old indebtedness	$1,648,500 00
New indebtedness	2,547,500 00
Total indebtedness	$4,206,000 00

STEPHEN D. GRIFFIN,
Clerk Superior Court.

It is evident from this showing, in order to keep within the County's resources, it will be necessary to curtail the expenses in every branch of the service. How this shall be accomplished without impairing the service will not only tax your best judgment, but will require your patient attention. The Circuit Judges can very materially aid in this direction by careful consideration of the question of how many assistants they allow the different departments under the provisions of the law.

This Board will be called on in the very near future to renew all its insurance policies now in force. This will require an additional outlay of about $20,000 for premiums.

LEGISLATIVE BUCCANEERING.

The last General Assembly passed an Act entitled, "An Act to tax gifts, legacies, inheritances," etc., which is now a law upon our statute books. This law provides that the tax so collected shall be paid to the State and is to be used for State purposes.

I do not wish to find fault with the Legislature that passed this law nor with the law itself, but I think this Board should ask the next General Assembly to repeal the above law and in its place pass an Act fixing a uniform tax upon all legacies or inheritances over the sum of $50,000 or $100,000, the tax so collected in each county in the State to be applied toward the support of the charitable institutions in the county, or to defraying the expenses the said county is called upon to pay to maintain its charges in charitable institutions. I see no reason why a tax raised in this manner would not be sufficient in time to bear the greater share of the cost of our charitable institutions, nor do I see why a tax raised in this manner should go to support the State government. It has so many other sources from which it can properly raise revenue, such as corporations, franchises, etc., that it should leave the sum derived from an inheritance or legacy tax to be expended as I have indicated.

A MERITORIOUS PROJECT.

In following the plan I have above outlined no poor person would be called upon to pay any sum or tax for the support of our poor unfortunates who become public charges, for certainly any heir receiving an inheritance of $50,000 or $100,000 could well afford to pay a reasonable sum as a tax, which would go for the purposes above stated, and no one would consider it any hardship to such heir; on the other hand, it being a notorious and conceded fact that the poor man is taxed much higher in proportion than the rich man, it necessarily follows that the poor pay a larger amount in proportion to their means than the rich toward the cost of maintaining our public charitable institutions.

By the method I have above suggested, the poor man will almost be entirely relieved from contributing to the maintenance of our public charitable institutions.

AN IMPORTANT PROPOSITION.

The City of Chicago, in my opinion, ought to bear some of the burdens which the County is now obliged to provide for; it should take care of the sick and maimed poor, and the State should take care of the insane and dependent children. With the limited revenues of the County we are called on to provide Court Houses and quarters for all County officers, a Jail, a Hospital, an Insane Asylum, a Poor House, a Morgue, and to pay for the running of all courts of record, State's Attorney's office, Coroner, Sheriff, and take care of the poor and insane and dependent children, pay for the clothing and necessaries for Cook County's inmates at the State charity institutions, and board for the prisoners sent to the Bridewell by the Criminal Court.

This Board should take action to secure an amendment to the present law by the Legislature in regard to fees and salaries of the State's Attorney's office, so that

CHARLES N. PETERS,
Chief Deputy Sheriff.

JOHN L. WHITMAN,
Jailor Cook County.

JAMES PEASE,
Sheriff of Cook County.

all moneys collected for the forfeiture of bail bonds be paid into the County Treasury. It is manifestly unjust that no accounting of this source of revenues should be made to the County.

In conclusion, I wish to thank the members of this Board for the prompt attendance at the meetings of this Board and their faithful discharge of their duties as members of the various committees, and their courtesy to me as President of the Board.

Referring to the estimate of our resources for the coming year, I trust it will be the aim of every member in considering the annual appropriation bill to see that every cent is placed where it will be of the most benefit to the citizens and taxpayers of Cook County and expended in a practical, business-like manner.

STATEMENT OF APPROPRIATIONS AND EXPENDITURES FOR SUPPLIES AND REPAIRS, 1895.

INSTITUTION OR OFFICE.	Amount Appropriated for Supplies and Repairs.	Amount Expended from Jan. 1 to June 30, 1895.	Amount Expended from July 1 to Dec. 1, 1895.	Balance Dec. 1, 1895.
Hospital and Detention Hospital	$155,000 00	$ 76,728 11	$ 55,065 85	$ 23,206 04
Dunning Institutions	220,000 00	128,096 55	77,098 59	14,804 86
County Agent	100,000 00	72,597 05	11,171 29	16,231 66
*Custodian Court House	50,000 00	35,824 20	9,293 60	4,782 20
*Custodian Criminal Court Building	16,000 00	4,713 48	5,455 36	5,831 16
Sheriff	12,000 00	7,722 48	4,277 52	....
Superintendent of Public Service	4,000 00	1,568 11	920 46	1,511 43
Commissioners and Comptroller	6,000 00	3,002 61	1,874 56	1,122 83
†State's Attorney	500 00 1,500 00	1,191 06	339 54	469 40
‡County Superintendent of Public Schools	2,404 93	746 48	490 87	1,167 58
Normal School	10,000 00	4,265 41	3,405 17	2,329 42
Coroner	2,000 00	353 54	369 76	1,276 70
Clerk of the Criminal Court	3,500 00	2,597 13	902 87	....
County Clerk and Clerk of the County Court	12,500 00	7,384 77	5,115 23	....
County Treasurer	8,000 00	4,984 67	956 59	2,058 74
Recorder	10,000 00	4,416 38	2,234 17	3,349 45
Clerk of the Circuit Court	8,500 00	3,854 15	4,645 85	....
Clerk of the Superior Court	8,000 00	3,001 62	2,967 80	2,030 58
Clerk of the Probate Court	4,500 00	3,139 54	1,139 31	221 15
Hospital Clinic Laboratory Fund	1,010 00	187 26	291 85	530 89
Normal School Library and Apparatus Fund	2,000 00	954 69	372 72	672 59
Civil Service Commission	250 00	....	186 18	63 85
County Attorney	2,600 00	1,460 64	528 06	611 30
		$368,789 93 189,203 20 82,271 80	$189,203 20	$ 83,271 80
Total	$640,264 93	$640,264 93		

*In February the sum of $16,000.00 was transferred from the Supply Fund of the Custodian of the Court House to Custodian of the Criminal Court Building.

†July 31, 1895, page 880, additional sum of $500.00 allowed for supplies.

‡Includes $904.93 brought forward from 1894 Supply Fund.

Office Superintendent Public Service
November 30, 1895.

JACOB J. KERN,
State's Attorney.

STATEMENT OF THE BUILDING FUND, 1895.

Date of Contract. Board Proceedings.	NAME OF CONTRACTOR.	DESCRIPTION OF WORK.	Amount of Contract.	Amount Certified to Comptroller for Payment.	Balance due on Contract.	REMARKS.
1895.						
Feb. 28..	Gutta Percha & Rubber Co...	14 hose racks, Criminal Court Bldg	$ 84 00	$ 84 00	....	
March 25	Carl Anderson Co...........	Removing old ice machine, Hospital	448 75	448 75	....	
April 22.	Hoffman Office File Co	Files, racks, galleries, railings, Criminal Court Clerk's office	3,346 50	3,346 50	....	
April 15.	Orris E. Taylor.............	Laundry extractor, Hospital	465 00	465 00	....	
April 29.	Edward J. Molloy...........	Masonry, new Jail	20,600 00	15,000 00	$ 5,600 00	
April 29.	Opfergelt & Turnes	Carpentry work, new Jail..........	5,772 00	800 00	4,972 00	
June 10..	Opfergelt & Turnes	Changes and alterations, new Jail...	573 00	300 00	273 00	
April 29.	Ernst Heldmeier	Cut stone work, new Jail..........	15,986 00	12,000 00	3,986 00	
April 29.	August Zander..............	Lathing and plastering, new Jail....	10,980 00	....	10,980 00	
April 29.	Robert B. Miller............	Roofing and sheet met. work, new Jail	5,485 00	....	5,485 00	
May 6...	Evans Marble Co............	Mosiac work, new Jail............	2,190 00	....	2,190 00	
April 29.	Simpson Bros...............	Concrete work, new Jail...........	6,100 00	....	6,100 00	
April 29.	Molin & Hoff...............	Structural iron work, new Jail......	11,300 00	8,500 00	2,800 00	
April 29.	Chicago Arch. Iron Works....	Ornamental iron work, new Jail.....	6,771 00	....	6,771 00	
April 29.	The Champion Iron Co.......	Window guards and doors, new Jail.	3,381 00	1,500 00	1,881 00	
April 29.	Altman & Samms...........	Elec. wiring, sp'k'g tubes, new Jail.	690 00	....	690 00	
April 29.	City of Chicago.............	Water pipe connections, Dunning ..	9,000 00	9,000 00	....	
April 22.	John T. McRoy.............	Repairing roof of the Jail	190 00	190 00	....	
May 13..	Robt. Gordon	9 boilers, Dunning institutions......	10,400 00	10,400 00	....	
May 20..	W. R. Thompson...........	....	....	....	....	
May 27..	W. R. Thompson...........	Repairing plumbing, Co. Hospital ..	10,986 00	9,000 00	1,986 00	
June 10..	Foss & Noble..............	Ventilating, County Hospital.......	11,237 00	6,000 00	5,237 00	
June 17..	Fenton Metallic Mfg. Co	File racks, Recorder's vaults........	5,288 00	5,288 00	....	
July 1...	County Treasurer...........	Commissions	38 73	38 73	....	
Jan. 28..	J. C. W. Rhode	Painting County Agent's office	100 00	100 00	....	
Jan. 28..	J. G. Lobstein	Partitions " " "	175 00	175 00	....	
July 1...	W. R. Thompson...........	Preliminary w'k, vault, Pro. Ct. Clk.	215 00	215 00	....	
July 1...	Fenton Metallic Mfg. Co.....	File racks & cases, Pro. Ct. Clk. vault.	882 00	882 00	....	
June 10..	The Congress Construction Co.	Gen'l repairs, boiler house, Dunning.	1,020 00	1,020 00	....	
....	A. G. Morey................	Commission of 5 per ct., 1st $100,000.	5,000 00	3,860 66 (for both A. G. Morey items)	2,389 34	
....	A. G. Morey................	" 2½ per ct. on $50,000.	1,250 00			
March 6.	Geo. C. Waterman..........	Survey, Jail lots	25 00	25 00	....	
Sept. 19.	Geo. C. Waterman..........	" block 7, Wolcot's addition..	25 00	25 00	....	
		Total......................	$ 150,003 98	$ 88,663 64	$ 61,340 34	
					88,663 64	
					$150,003 98	

Office Superintendent of Public Service, November 30, 1895.

SAMUEL B. CHASE,
Recorder of Cook County.

STATEMENT OF CLAIMS CERTIFIED TO BE PAID OUT OF THE CONTINGENT FUND, 1895.

Date Authorized	NAME.	KIND OF WORK.	Amount Contract.	Amount Paid.	Balance Due.	REMARKS.
1895.						
Jan. 28	Wm. G. Wood	Insurance premium, Co. Agt's stock	$ 57 00	$ 57 00		
Jan. 28	P. G. Gardner	" " " "	92 50	92 50		
	Dr. Archibald Church	Expert testimony, Criminal Court	75 00	75 00		State's Attorney, req. No. 361½.
	Dr. W. C. Caldwell	" " " "	100 00	100 00		" " " 367.
March 18	E. J. Walton	Reporting trial, Daniel Moore	27 25	27 25		Sec. 3, Bd. pc'ds., March 8, 1895.
March 18	E. J. Walton	" " Daniel O'Counor	100 87	100 87		" " " "
March 18	E. J. Walton	" Grand Jury, Nov., 1894	176 65	176 65		Judge Chetlain's Court.
March 19	T. J. Bluthardt	Expert testimony, Criminal Court	350 00	350 00		State's Attorney, req. No. 405.
	Jas. Mulcahy	For State's Attoruey, Criminal Court	33 50	33 50		" " " 395.
	D. J. C. Spray	" " " "	125 00	125 00		" " " 385.
	Dr. J. H. Stowell	" " " "	75 00	75 00		" " " 380.
	Dr. Frances W. McNamara	" " " "	75 00	75 00		" " " 363.
	Dr. J. R. Corbus	" " " "	75 00	75 00		" " " 359.
	Wyckoff, Seamans & Benedict	" " " "	14 25	14 25		" " " 384.
	Dr. A. J. Baxter	" " " "	100 00	100 00		" " " 356.
	Dr. Oscar J. Price	" " " "	75 00	75 00		" " " 357.
	E. J. Walton	" " " "	231 86	231 86		" " " 362.
	E. J. Walton	" " " "	541 97	541 97		" " " 397.
	E. J. Waltou	" " " "	34 87	34 87		" " " 393.
	E. J. Walton	" " " "	124 12	124 12		" " " 392.
	James M. Purcell	" " " "	94 63	94 63		" " " 386.
	E. J. Walton	Trial Patrick Shea, " "	184 50	184 50		Sec. 3, Bd. pc'ds., March 18, 1895.
	E. J. Walton	" Edna Brown, " "	32 57	32 57		" " " "
	E. J. Walton	" Lupold, " "	54 41	54 41		" " " "
	E. J. Walton	" Ellington, " "	180 92	180 92		" " " "
	E. J. Walton	" Reseps, " "	141 34	141 34		" " " "
	E. J. Walton	" Johu Fowler, " "	17 50	17 50		" " " "
	E. J. Walton	" Oscar Felsch, " "	109 75	109 75		" " " "
	C. E. Bush	Plat of bldgs., People *vs.* Schmack	15 00	15 00		
	E. S. Bottum	State's Attoruey's expense	2 00	2 00		Par. 4, Mar. 18, Sta. Atty, req. 396.
	Henrietta Snell	Tax, 1891, refunded	13 50	13 50		March 18, 1895, Board pc'ds.
	A. J. Snell	" "	15 84	15 84		" " "
	H. L. Gloss	" "	20 22	20 22		" " "
	Norwegian Evangelical Lutheran St. John's Church	Tax, 1893, refunded	2 57	2 57		April 8, 1895, "
	James Muller	" "	7 66	7 66		" " "
	J. H. Heald	" "	1 92	1 92		" " "
	Dr. Hy. L. Tollman	Expert services, Judge Dunne's Ct.	55 00	55 00		
	J. J. Kelly Coal Co.	Coal deliv. to Dunning after July, 1894	2,071 07	2,071 07		
	R. Robertson	Plumbing, Detention Hospital, 1892.	45 80	45 80		Par. 11, April 22, 1895.
	Chicago Carpet Co.	Carpet 5th and 6th floors Cr. Ct. bldg.	159 60	159 60		" 7, May 13, 1895.
	Olaf Severson	Services Board of Canvassers	30 00	30 00		April 2, 1895.
	Chicago Gas Light & Coke Co.	Con. Deteu. Hosp. with gas main, 1892	98 20	98 20		Sec. 6, June 9, 1895.
	J. T. Foster	Map County Farm	175 00	175 00		Page 259, February 25, 1895.
	Officer McGuire	Services State's Attorney's office	10 00	10 00		Sta. Atty. req. 388, March 19, 1895.

W. D. S. ANDERSON,
Assistant County Treasurer.

D. H. KOCHERSPERGER.
County Treasurer.

....	Geo. Kersten	Serv. canv. election ret. April 2, 1895.	$ 30 00	$ 30 00	....	....
....	Merle & Heaney Mfg. Co	Furniture, Criminal Court Building.	122 50	122 50	....	May 13, 1895.
....	Arthur G. Morey	Plans of construction, Co. Hospital	400 00	400 00	....	Sec. 13, April 8, 1895, p. 396.
....	Livingston W'house & V'n Co.	Sleigh, jurors, Peo. *vs.* Moran-Healey.	15 00	15 00	....	July 15 and 31, 1895, pp. 749. 831.
....	Humiston, Keeling & Co	Extra supply pipe, County Jail	3 15	3 15	....	Resolution, July 8, 1895, p. 725.
....	Heath & Milligan Mfg. Co	" " "	20 00	20 00	....	" " " "
....	L. Wolff Mfg. Co	" " "	119 47	119 47	....	" " " "
....	Syphon Furnace Co	Smoke device, County Hospital	50 00	50 00	....	Sec. 5, June 24, 1895, p. 670.
....	Chi. Rubber & Mill Sup. Co.	Steam fittings, Dunning	51 75	51 75	....	Resolution, July 31, 1895, p. 832.
....	John Davis Co	" "	31 09	31 09	....	" " " "
....	I. F. Harms & Co	" "	36 00	36 00	....	" " " "
....	Bhi. Elevator and Repair Co.	Repairs, Hospital elevators	1,014 00	1,014 00	....	Sec. 3, July 15, pp. 749 and 760.
....	John Healey	Laying water pipes, Dunning	3,498 44	3,498 44	....	" 6, " 15 and 22, pp. 749, 774.
....	W. R. Thompson	Plumbing and slop sinks, Co. Hosp.	383 00	383 00	....	" 6, " 30, p. 817.
....	J. B. Clow & Sons	Fittings, new boilers, Dunning, 7 bills.	666 41	666 41	....	Resolution, July 29, p. 814.
....	Western Electric Co	Wiring County Hospital	818 00	818 00	....	July 22, 1895, pp. 749 and 782.
....	John Healey	Extra labor going under steam pipes.	150 00	150 00	....	Sec. 9, Sept. 16, 1895.
....	Gunthorpe-Warren Ptg. Co	Blanks, Civil Service Commission	6 00	6 00	....	Req. No. 3, Civil Service Com.
....	Roy S. Gaskell	Asst. Co. Elec'n. Sept. and Oct., 1895.	130 00	130 00	....	Sec. 5, Sept. 16, 1895, p. 900.
....	Julius Speyer	Balance commissions architect, 1893.	476 00	476 00	....	Sept. 30, 1895, p. 936.
....	John Davis Co	Angle valves and fittings, Dunning	36 45	36 45	....	Req. 2823, passed Sept. 20, 1895.
....	J. B. Clow & Sons	" " " "	20 76	20 76	....	" " "
....	J. M. W. Jones, Sta. & Ptg. Co.	Civil Service blanks	5 63	5 63	....	Civil Service Req. 3.
....	Chi., Mad. & Northern R. R.	Taxes paid in error 1892 and 1893	161 25	161 25	....	Bd. pc'ds. Sept. 23, 1895, p. 918.
....	John Healey	Laying additional water pipe, Dun'g	2,585 05	2,585 05	....	" July 31, " p. 829.
....	John Davis Co	Fittings " " "	58 75	58 75	....	" " " "
....	J. B. Clow & Sons	Two 6-inch water meters	1,150 00	1,150 00	....	" Sept. 23, 30, pp. 921, 940.
....	Chicago Scale Co	Twenty-ton scale, Criminal Ct. bldg.	250 00	250 00	....	" " 3, p. 851.
....	Edward Edson	Decorating interior Adm'n Hosp. blg.	990 00	750 00	$ 240 00	" " 23, 1895, pp. 919, 739, 935, 750.
....	Troy Laundry Machin'y Co	Washing machine, Dunning Ins	375 00	375 00	....	" " 16, 1895, p. 901.
....	O'Donnell & Wilder	Repairing Jail roof	50 00	50 00	....	" Oct. 21, 1895, p. 997.
....	W. R. Thompson	4-inch gate valve, Hospital elevators.	16 00	16 00	....	Sec. 3, July 15, 1895, p. 654.
....	Wm. Sullivan	Steam heating, old Jail Building	1,450 00	1,450 00	....	Bd. pc'ds., Sept. 16, 1895, p. 904.
....	J. M. W. Jones Sta & Ptg. Co.	Stationery and blanks, Clerk Cr. Ct.	280 79	280 79	....	1 sundry req., Clerk Crim. Court.
....	Eureka Fire Hose Co	1,000 feet fire hose, Dunning	350 00	350 00	....	Bd. pc'ds. Sept. 30, p. 939.
....	J. M. W. Jones Sta. & Ptg. Co	Calendars, Criminal Court	90 00	90 00	....	Clerk Crim. Ct., req. No. 215.
....	W. D. Kerfoot	Rent rooms, Chicago Opera House	100 00	100 00	....	Oct. 21, 1895, p. 996.
....	Adam Davidson	Expense of transp. election booths	2 87	2 87	....	Harlem precinct, County.
....	Hy. R. Worthington	Fire pump, Dunning	1,875 00	....	1,875 00	Sept. 23, 1895, p. 923.
....	Opfergelt & Turnes	Repairing Hospital stairs	297 00	....	297 00	Sec. 10, Oct. 21, p. 996.
....	E. C. Cook & Bro	Polling booths for County	97 50	....	97 50	" " p. 996.
....	Wm. Sullivan	Removing old heating plant, Jail	200 00	....	200 00	Sec. 9, Nov. 11, 1895.
....	Edward J. Malloy	Excavations foundations, Jail	2,000 00	....	2,000 00	June 24, 1895.
....	W. R. Thompson	P'lb'g, gas fit'g and sewerage, Jail	1,575 00	....	1,575 00	May 20, 1895.
		Total	....	$ 21,777 20	$ 6,284 50	
					21,777 20	
		Total	$ 28,061 70	....	$ 28,061 70	

All of which is respectfully submitted,

D. D. HEALY, President.

ORRIN N. CARTER,
Judge County Court.

RULES OF THE BOARD OF COOK COUNTY COMMISSIONERS.

MEETINGS.

Rule 1—Regular meetings shall be held on the first Monday of December, January, February, March, June and September in each year at 2 p. m. At the hour of meeting the President shall call the Board to order and instruct the Clerk to call the roll and note the absentees.

Rule 2—A majority of all the members shall constitute a quorum for the transaction of business. Should a quorum not be present, the meeting shall stand adjourned from day to day until a quorum is obtained.

Rule 3—The regular order of business, unless otherwise directed by the Board, shall be as follows:

(1) Reading and approving the records of the proceedings of the last meeting.
(2) Unfinished business.
(3) Communications and petitions.
(4) Reports from standing committees.
(5) Reports from special committees.
(6) Resolutions and motions.

PRESIDENT OF THE BOARD.

Rule 4—It shall be the duty of the President to enforce all the rules for the government of the several Institutions and Departments of Cook County, and the neglect or refusal of any officer or employe to observe said rules shall be sufficient cause for the suspension or removal of said officer or emyloye by the President. And any vacancy so created shall be filled in the manner in which the appointment was originally made, provided nothing herein shall be construed to evade the rules of Civil Service.

He shall call special meetings of the Board whenever, in his opinion, the same may be necessary, or upon the written request of five members of the Board, and he shall preside at all meetings of the Board, and generally perform all the duties of a presiding officer.

He shall preserve order and decorum; shall decide all questions of order—subject, however, to an appeal from his decision; shall refuse to entertain any proposition involving the expenditure of money unless the same is reduced to writing, with the signature in full of the member offering the same endorsed thereon; shall order a call of the yeas and nays upon all appropriation resolutions, and upon all propositions whereby any liability, directly or indirectly, may be created, and upon all other propositions, whenever the same is demanded by any member of the Board; and whenever a report of a committee or any proposition involving the expenditure of more than $500 has been divided for the purpose of considering it item by item, and after the last item has been disposed of, he shall, whether a motion to that effect be made or not, put the question: Shall the report (resolution or motion, as the case may be) be adopted as a whole? And thereupon he shall order a call of the yeas and nays.

He shall have the same privilege of voting as other Commissioners, but he shall not have a deciding vote in case of a tie upon any proposition upon which he has voted as Commissioner.

He shall personally examine all requisitions for supplies, and if, in his judgment, any of the articles mentioned are unnecessary or extravagant, he shall strike them out and report such action to Public Service Committee for their action, and the sub-committees of the different institutions and departments shall limit the supplies for the various institutions and departments of the County, so that the several appropriations shall not become exhausted before the close of each fiscal year.

He shall, from time to time, personally inspect the books, papers and accounts of the Superintendent of Public Service and of the Comptroller, and in case of the failure of either of said officers to conduct his office in a proper manner, or to comply with the provisions of law or rules of the Board defining their respective duties, he shall promptly report the same to the Board.

He shall sign all contracts for supplies, material and work, after the same has been approved by the Board. *Provided, however*, that no contract shall be executed or liability incurred until he shall have ascertained that there is sufficient money in the proper fund to liquidate such contract or liability.

He shall, on or before the 31st day of December of each year, by and with the advice and consent of the Board, appoint a Superintendent of Public Service, a Superintendent of the Institutions at Dunning, including the Poor Farm, a Warden of the County Hospital, a County Agent, a County Attorney, a County Physician, a County Architect, a Custodian of the Court House, a Custodian of the Criminal Court Building, and a Committee Clerk of the County Board, all of whom shall be subject to these rules.

He shall appoint the Chairman of the Committee on Public Service, and shall appoint all Standing Committees of the Board, except the Committee on Public Service, subject to the approval of the Board, and shall be ex-officio a member of all Committees. And shall have such other powers and perform such other duties as are provided by law.

In the absence of the President the Board shall elect a presiding officer *pro tempore*, who shall, during such absence or inability, possess all the powers and perform all the duties imposed upon said President by law and by these rules.

COMMITTEE ON FINANCE.

Rule 5—There shall be a Committee on Finance, to consist of five members, and a Committee on Roads and Bridges, consisting of three members to be appointed by the President, subject to the approval of the Board. It shall be the duty of the Finance Committee to prepare the annual appropriation resolution, in and by which shall be appropriated such sums of money as may be necessary to defray all the necessary expenses and liabilities of the County to be paid and incurred during the fiscal year; and said resolution shall specify in detail the several objects and purposes for which such appropriations are made, and the amount appropriated for each object or purpose; said resolution shall be submitted to the Board for adoption at a meeting thereof to be held prior to the 31st day of March in each year. It shall also be the duty of said Committee, together with the President, to superintend and direct the Comptroller in the management of his office, and see that he shall open and keep in a clear, methodical manner, a complete set of books, which shall show in detail every appropriation for the fiscal

F. S. BAIRD,
Chairman Board of Election Commissioners.

ISAAC N. POWELL,
Chief Clerk Board of Election Commissioners.

W. W. WHEELOCK,
Attorney Board of Election Commissioners.

year, and also the actual and estimated receipts from every source of revenue, and such books shall be kept so as to show, at all times, during the fiscal year, the amount of money remaining in each fund unexpended. And said Committee shall systematically examine all books, papers, vouchers, contracts, bonds, receipts and all other matters in said office pertaining to the finances of the County.

All claims against the County which have been audited by the Comptroller shall be referred to the Finance Committee, and its action thereon shall be specifically reported in writing to the Board for final action.

Said Committee shall direct the Comptroller to furnish monthly to the Board statements of the condition of each fund, showing the amount appropriated and the amount expended, and the balance remaining, to the end that no indebtedness shall be created in excess of the several amounts appropriated. All matters pertaining to taxes and financial affairs of the County generally shall be referred to the Finance Committee.

COMMITTEE ON PUBLIC SERVICE.

Rule 6—There shall be a committee on Public Service, which shall comprise all the members of the Board, the chairman of which shall be ex-officio member of all sub-committees thereof. It shall be the duty of the Committee on Public Service, subject to the approval of the Board, to devise rules for the government of the several County institutions and departments of public service, which shall include a system of visitation and inspection by said Committee, and for this purpose there may be appointed from its members the requisite number of Sub-Committees.

Said Committee on Public Service shall superintend the office of Superintendent of Public Service, and see that he keeps proper books of accounts, vouchers, etc., and shall, from time to time, inspect the same; it shall, subject to the approval of the Board, make all needful rules and regulations for the proper conduct of his office.

All supplies shall be purchased and issued to the several institutions and departments of the County only upon requisitions, which shall be made in triplicate, and no requisition calling for supplies exceeding the sum of $500 shall be divided by any officer or committee for the purpose of enabling such officer or committee to purchase the same without having first received the approval of the Board.

SUB-COMMITTEES OF PUBLIC SERVICE COMMITTEE.

Rule 7—The Chairman of the Public Service Committee shall appoint the following sub-committees of the Committee on Public Service, to-wit: Insane Asylum and Poor House, County Hospital, Outdoor Relief, Jail and Criminal Court, Court House, Coroner and Morgue, Building, Judiciary, Educational, Stationery and Printing, and City Relations.

COMMITTEE CLERK.

Rule 8—The Committee Clerk shall keep a record of the proceedings of all committee meetings. Said record shall show the names of the members present, and those voting for and against the adoption of all reports; and shall also contain a complete statement of the amount of all the bids, and by whom, and for what made, which have been considered by any committee. Said record shall be open at all times to the inspection of the members of the Board and to the public.

All the reports of committees shall be in writing and contain the facts of the matter submitted, with such recommendations as may be deemed proper, and the report of the Committee on Finance shall be signed by the members of the committee who approve the same. And the report of the Committee on Public Service shall be signed by the chairman of such committee only. Any member or members may submit a minority report, either upon the whole or any part of any report presented.

All matters referred to a committee shall be reported back to the next meeting or adjourned meeting of the Board, and in case of a failure to so report, the subject matter may be recalled by a majority vote of the Board, and acted upon, the same as if it had been reported by the committee.

COUNTY BOARD.

Rule 9—Any member who desires to speak shall rise from his seat and address himself to the President, and shall confine himself strictly to the proposition pending before the Board, and avoid personalities.

Rule 10—No member shall speak more than twice nor longer than five minutes on the same question without leave of the Board. But in a question of appeal no member shall speak more than once.

Upon a call of the yeas and nays, no member shall speak more than two minutes in explanation of his vote.

Rule 11—When a question is put to the Board, every member present shall vote, unless excused by the Board or personally interested therein.

Rule 12—After a motion has been stated by the President, or read by the Clerk, it shall be deemed the property of the Board, but may be withdrawn at any time before amendment.

Rule 13—If the question under debate contains several distinct propositions, any member may call for a division, but such questions shall not be finally disposed of until it has been submitted as a whole. And when a blank has been filled and different sums or times proposed, the question shall first be put upon the largest sum and longest time.

Rule 14—When a question is before the board no motion shall be in order but these: First, to fix the time to which the Board shall adjourn when it adjourns; second, to adjourn; third, to lay on table; fourth, the previous question; fifth, to postpone indefinitely; sixth, to postpone to a certain time; seventh, to commit; eighth, to amend; and these motions shall be privileged and have precedence in the order in which they are made to succeed each other by this rule. And the motion to adjourn, to lay on the table and for the previous question, shall be decided, without debate.

Rule 15—A motion to adjourn shall always be in order, except, first, when a member is in possession of the floor; second, when the yeas and nays are being called; third, when the members are voting; fourth, when adjournment was the last preceding motion; or, fifth, when it has been decided that the previous question shall be taken, and the "previous question" shall be as follows: "Shall the main question be now put?"

Rule 16—The effect of the main question being ordered shall be to put to an end all debate and bring the Board to a direct vote, first upon all amendments pending, and then on the main question.

Rule 17—A member who votes with the prevailing side, or any Commissioner who was absent at the time the vote was taken, may move a reconsideration, but no such motion shall be in order after the expiration of the next meeting of the Board.

Rule 18—All resolutions or motions whereby any money shall be appropriated, or by virtue of which any contract shall be made, or any act done which may directly or indirectly, or in any manner whatever, create any pecuniary liability on the part of the County, shall be submitted in writing, with the signature in full of the member offering the same; and no such proposition, if the amount involved exceeds the sum of $500, shall be put upon its final passage until after a reference to one of the standing committees of the Board and a report from such committee to the Board at a subsequent meeting thereof; and the vote upon all propositions involving the expenditure of money, whether for more or less than $500, shall be by yeas and nays, and the result thereof shall be entered upon the records of the Board.

Rule 19—The roll shall be called and the yeas and nays taken and entered upon the record upon the demand of any member. All contracts for supplies, material and work shall first be approved by the Board and signed by the President, Superintendent of Public Service and Comptroller. All bonds taken for the faithful performance of contracts, and all bonds given by County officers and employes, shall be referred to the Finance Committee to inquire into the sufficiency of the sureties, and after they have been approved by the Finance Committee and confirmed by the Board, they shall be filed in the office of the Comptroller as provided by law.

Rule 20—Any proposition for the purchase or sale of real estate shall be considered by the Board in open session, and all deeds and contracts for the same shall receive the approval of the President and two-thirds of all the members elected to the County Board before becoming binding upon the County.

Rule 21—All communications or resolutions presented by a member of the Board upon which any action is taken, shall be printed in the Proceedings of the Board, and all bonds, contracts, communications from contractors and County officers, and all estimates of architects approved by the Board, and all requisitions for supplies shall be printed in the current Proceedings.

Rule 22—No receipt, order for goods, requisitions, vouchers, contracts, bills, bonds, coupons, or papers of any sort used by an officer, committee or the Board, shall be destroyed, but after being used or paid shall be indorsed to that effect and filed with the Clerk for safe-keeping until the same shall be ordered to be destroyed by a resolution of the Board, and such destruction shall be done as directed by the Board.

Rule 23—No person not a member or ex-member of the Board, or an officer or an employe thereof, shall be allowed inside the railing or upon the floor of the Board while the same is in session, unless by permission of the Board or the presiding officer thereof.

Rule 24—The rules of parliamentary practice comprised in "Roberts' Rules of Order" shall govern the Board in all cases in which they are applicable and not inconsistent with the standing rules and orders of the Board.

Rule 25—The Superintendent of the County Institutions at Dunning shall reside in one of the said Institutions free of rent and household expenses for his own family, and shall be responsible for the management of said Institutions, including the Poor Farm.

The Warden of the County Hospital shall reside at the County Hospital free of rent and household expenses for his own family, and shall be held responsible for the management of the Hospital.

They shall regulate visits, discipline employes, and shall see that every department is properly conducted, and that the strictest economy is practiced consistent with efficient service and the welfare of the patients.

ESTIMATES AND PAY-ROLLS.

Rule 26—The Warden of the County Hospital, the Superintendent of the Insane Asylum and Poor House, the County Agent, the Custodian of the Court House and the Custodian of the Criminal Court Building, shall submit to the President a complete list of all employes under them, the position and amount of salary, as provided in the annual appropriation bill, and the President shall cause a record to be kept of said employes under proper headings, the position and amount of salary; and the Comptroller shall keep a like record, and the pay-rolls submitted by the heads of the various institutions and departments shall correspond with said records.

Suspensions for inefficiency, incapacity and for violation of rules shall be reported to the President at once, who in turn shall notify the Comptroller. Any violation of the foregoing by the head of any department or institution shall be sufficient cause for his removal. The President's record of appointments shall be open at all times for inspection by the Commissioners.

Rule 27—The heads of all departments and institutions of Cook County, including the County officers, shall, on or before the 31st day of December, in each year, submit to the County Comptroller itemized estimate of the amount of money required to meet the expenses of their several departments and offices during the succeeding year, commencing January 1, and shall also submit a statement of the receipts and expenditures of their several offices and departments during the preceding year. All officers and heads of departments shall attach to their several pay-rolls, when presented for audit, an affidavit in the following form, viz: "——— ——— ——— being duly sworn, says that this pay-roll is true and correct, and that the several items herein mentioned are in accordance with the order of the County Board, and also with the list of salaries adopted by the County Board for the period in which the service as charged was rendered, and that the persons whose names appear on said pay-roll are either native or naturalized American citizens, or have in good faith declared their intention to become such, as required by an Act of the General Assembly of the State of Illinois, approved June 1, 1889, in force July 1, 1889, or are exempt from the operation of said Act by reason of age or sex."

REQUISITIONS.

Rule 28—The heads of all departments and institutions of the County, including the County officers, shall make application to the Superintendent of Public Service for all supplies, which by law the County is required to furnish; such application shall be made by requisition, at such time and in such manner as the Superintendent of Public Service may prescribe, unless otherwise provided in the rules, or by special order of the County Board.

All requisitions for supplies shall show the quantity of goods on hand, and the quantity received and distributed since the first day of the month in which the requisition is made. Failure to fill out the blanks prepared for this purpose shall be deemed sufficient cause for suspension or removal.

In all cases where requisitions are submitted, calling for goods which can be purchased only by samples, the officer or department making the requisition must submit to the Superintendent of Public Service samples of the articles required.

From the date of the adoption of these rules no indebtedness or liability contracted in any other manner than as herein specified, by any officer of the County, whether elected by the people, or appointed by the County Board, shall be recognized or paid, unless it shall appear that the officer contracting the same had authority, by law, so to do.

RECORDS AND REPORTS.

Rule 29—The officers of every institution and department under the control of the County Board shall keep accurate books of account, in a clear and methodical manner, under the direction of the Superintendent of Public Service, so as to correspond with the books kept in his office, and such books shall be open to the inspection of members of the Board and the Superintendent of Public Service at any and at all times.

The General Superintendent of the Institutions at Dunning — including the Poor Farm, the Warden of the County Hospital, the County Agent, and the County Physician shall each keep a register, in which shall be recorded the name of each patient, inmate or applicant for relief; the sex, age, residence, occupation, nativity, and, if sick or disabled, the disease or cause of disability, together with such other items of information as the President of the Board may direct. In all institutions to which this rule will apply the register must also show the number or letter of the ward and the number of the bed occupied by the party named, as well as the names of such relatives or friends as are to be notified in case of death. The records must also show all births and deaths occurring in the several institutions, and in all cases of death the relatives and friends of the deceased must be immediately notified.

On the first day of each and every month the General Superintendent of the Institutions at Dunning—including the Poor Farm, and the Wardens of the Cook County Hospital and the Detention Hospital, shall report to the County Board full information as to number of admissions, discharges, deaths, and still remaining in their several institutions, and the County agent shall report the number of applications for relief, the number refused, and the number to whom relief was granted during the preceding month. The County agent shall also report, on or before the fifth day of every month, all expenditures of the preceding month, together with the amount of supplies on hand, received and distributed during the preceding month, and the number of persons to whom relief had been granted.

The heads of the several departments named, shall each, on the first day of December of each year, make an annual report, which shall be a summary of the monthly and weekly reports as above specified.

The persons in charge of the different departments and institutions of the County shall make reports, not otherwise specified, at such times and in such manner as the President of the County Board may direct.

BONDS.

Rule 30—The Superintendent of Public Service shall, within ten days after the date of his appointment, file with the County Board a good and sufficient bond in the penal sum of $50,000; the General Superintendent of the institutions at Dunning—including the Poor Farm, and the Warden of the County Hospital, each in the penal sum of $10,000, and the County Agent and the County Physician in the penal sum of $10,000, all conditional on the faithful discharge of their several duties.

GENERAL POWERS OF OFFICERS.

Rule 31—No officer, employe or assistant in the employ of Cook County, shall accept or receive from any source whatever any fees, emoluments or perquisities or presents, directly or indirectly, other than the salary or other compensation designated by this Board or such as is authorized by the statutes of the State of Illinois for any services rendered or to be rendered in the discharge of any duties connected or incident to the position he or she holds while in the employment of the County.

All heads of departments shall so regulate their expenditures so that the expenses for any year shall not exceed the amounts of the appropriation for that year.

Superintendents and heads of departments shall make such rules and regulations for the government of their respective officers and institutions as may be approved by the President of the County Board and the committee in charge.

ADMISSION TO INSTITUTIONS.

Rule 32—The admission of inmates to the Poor House shall be only upon the order of the County Agent and the County Physician, or the Supervisor of the town wherein the applicant resides.

No person shall be admitted as an inmate of the Insane Asylum unless committed by due process of law.

No person shall be admitted as an inmate of the Hospital who is known to be financially able to provide for himself, and whenever it is ascertained that such persons are being cared for they shall be discharged.

PROHIBITION OF LIQUOR.

Rule 33—Any employe, attendant or inmate of the Poor House, Insane Asylum or Hospital who introduces liquor, or who shall be found under the influence of liquor within or upon the grounds of the Institution to which he belongs, or who shall disturb the house by quarreling, using profane or abusive language, or shall behave with disrespect to the officers or employes, or act immorally in any respect, shall be immediately discharged.

HEADS OF DEPARTMENTS AND INSTITUTIONS.

Rule 34—It shall be the duty of the heads of various departments and institutions to prescribe the several duties of the employes under them; they may suspend such employes at their pleasure for inefficiency or inability to perform the duties for which they were employed and shall report the same to the President. They shall have full charge of all business matters pertaining to the management of their respective departments and institutions, being subject only to the statutes of the

State of Illinois, and such rules, regulations and orders as the Board of County Commissioners have in these matters determined or may hereafter make. It shall be the duty of the Superintendent of the Dunning Institutions, so far as possible, to prevent the escape of patients entrusted to his care, but in the event of an escape, immediate search must be made until the patient is found and returned. He shall allow only patients and employes at the Dunning Institutions to participate in the weekly dance or other entertainments at the Asylum given for the benefit of patients.

Patients and inmates of all the Institutions of the County must be treated with humanity and care. Unnecessary force shall not be employed in any case, and force shall not be used at all except in extreme cases, and all such cases must be immediately reported in writing to the chief officer of such department. Any attendant known to have struck or abused a patient or inmate, or who shall have failed to report as above shall be immediately discharged.

COUNTY PHYSICIAN.

Rule 35—The County Physician shall reside at the Detention Hospital and give proper medical attendance to patients at that Institution, including attention at Court. He shall supervise the transfer of patients from the Detention Hospital to the Insane Asylum. It shall also be his duty to report to the Warden any improper conduct or neglect of duty on the part of any attendant or employe at the Detention Hospital.

He shall, with the advice and co-operation of the Sheriff, have a general oversight of the sanitary regulations of the County Jail, and give all necessary medical or surgical attention to individuals confined therein.

COUNTY FARMER.

Rule 36—The Farmer shall reside on the Farm, in such building as the County Board may direct. It shall be his duty to see that the farm is well cultivated. He shall have control of everything pertaining to the management of the farm, subject to the approval of the General Superintendent, including the barns and stock belonging to the Institutions at Dunning. He shall be furnished by the General Superintendent of the Institutions at Dunning, including the Poor Farm, such inmates of the Insane Asylum and Poor House as are able to perform the work required, and such numbers as he may be able to use and, upon the order of the Board of County Commissioners, the President may furnish him such additional assistants as may be required. He shall transfer patients between the railroad stations and the Institutions at Dunning, and do such other work in the line of teaming as may from time to time be directed by the Sub-Committee on Poor House and Insane Asylum. He shall not allow the County teams to be used on the road for amusement. He shall make application to the General Superintendent of the Institutions at Dunning, including the Poor Farm, for such supplies as may be required for the use of the farm or barns, and shall keep an accurate account thereof.

He shall, by and with the advice of the Committee in charge, decide upon the number of horses to be used for farm labor, and such as are to be used for the service of the institutions, and select such as are to be sold and dispose of them to the best possible advantage.

In the management of the farm he shall give preference to the raising of such vegetables and produce as are required for use at the institutions, and in the cultivation of which the largest number of inmates can be most profitably employed. He shall see that the crops are properly harvested, and shall inform the Superintendent from time to time what supplies he can furnish, in order that the same may be used and not allowed to waste on the ground.

He shall keep an account of the supplies furnished him for the use of the farm, and also of the crop raised and delivered to the institutions. He shall take a receipt in every case for all supplies delivered, and shall charge the same to the proper institution at the market price, and report the same, with his receipts, to the Superintendent of Public Service for information.

MONTHLY REPORTS TO SUPERINTENDENT OF PUBLIC SERVICE:

Rule 37—The heads of the different charitable institutions shall, on or before the fifth day of every month, submit to the Superintendent of Public Service, to be by him reported to the County Board, a statement of the expenditures of the institutions under their charge for the preceding month, and they shall also furnish a statement containing a list, in alphabetical order, of all the goods on hand at the beginning of the month, the amount received, the amount consumed and the amount on hand at the end of the month; and they shall also submit a statement showing the number of inmates during the month.

SUPERINTENDENT OF PUBLIC SERVICE.

Rule 38—It shall be the duty of the Superintendent of Public Service to purchase all the supplies for the several departments and institutions of the County, in the manner provided by law, except in those cases where express authority is conferred by statute on some other officer so to do.

In the month of December in each year, between the 10th and 15th day thereof, he shall advertise for bids for meat, milk, beer, clothing, bread, ice and yeast, to be furnished the several County institutions, and also for dieting jurors, removing garbage, and advertising, for the period of one year, beginning on the first day of January next following.

In the month of November in each year, between the 10th and 15th day thereof, he shall advertise for bids for Printing Proceedings of the Board for one year, beginning on the first Monday in December next following.

In the month of June of each year, between the 10th and 15th day thereof, he shall advertise for bids for all the coal required by the County for one year, beginning July 1 next following.

Between the 15th and 20th days of the months of December, March, June and September, in each year, he shall advertise for bids for all other supplies needed by the County (except such articles as are known as daily supplies) for each quarter, beginning the first day of January, April, July and October, except as herein otherwise provided.

All supplies not included in contracts made for one year shall be included in the contracts made for three months, when the quantity and kind can be accurately described, and also when bids can be intelligently made from samples submitted. Requisitions for contract goods in cases of emergency may be filled by the Superintendent of Public Service, upon the approval of the President, without submitting the same to the Board.

Supplies not included in contracts, when the estimated cost of the quantity named in the requisition is more than $100 but does not exceed $500, may be purchased by the Superintendent without advertising, on bids solicited from business houses dealing in the articles called for.

When the estimated cost of the goods contained in any one requisition does not exceed $100, they shall be purchased by the Superintendent of Public Service at the lowest market price.

When the estimated cost of such goods exceed the sum of $500, and the articles are not covered by any contract, the bids therefor must be submitted to the Board of Commissioners for action.

All advertised bids, excepting those for quarterly supplies, shall be presented to this Board, and opened in open board meeting in the presence of all such bidders as desire to be present.

All bids for quarterly supplies shall be opened by the Superintendent of Public Service, in the presence of the Board of Commissioners, and of such bidders as desire to be present.

The Superintendent of Public Service shall in no case supply goods or articles of any description to any officer, department or institution, except upon a requisition submitted in the manner provided for in the Standing Rules of this Board, nor shall any contractor be permitted to deliver supplies under any contract upon the order of any other officer or person than the Superintendent of Public Service.

The Superintendent of Public Service shall keep accurate books of account, under the direction of the President, so that the several amounts expended may be deducted from the amount appropriated for each specific purpose, and he shall keep the heads of the several institutions and departments fully advised, so that their expenditures shall not exceed the amounts appropriated. It shall also be his duty to direct in what manner the books shall be kept in the several institutions, and also in the office of the County Agent, so far as they relate to supplies, and he shall supervise and inspect the same from time to time, and report to the Board of Commissioners the result of such investigations.

He shall also keep a daily record of all bills for goods delivered, and after certifying to the correctness of such bills, he shall deliver them to the Comptroller.

He shall also have tests made, from time to time (when in his judgment it is necessary), of any contract supplies furnished to any of the institutions of Cook County, in order to determine whether or not such supplies are being furnished in accordance with the terms of the contract.

COUNTY ATTORNEY.

Rule 39—The County Attorney shall be the legal adviser of the County Board, and shall have charge of all suits at law or in equity, for or against the County, and shall be entitled to such assistants as the Board of County Commissioners shall provide.

He shall systematize the work of his office and assign to his several assistants their respective duties, and be prepared to report to the Board of County Commissioners the condition of his office, the state of the work therein, or any department thereof, or any special matter pertaining thereto, whensoever required by said Board.

The assistants in his office shall be severally responsible to the County Attorney, and to the Board of County Commissioners for the conduct of the suits and other matters assigned to them, and the faithful performance of their respective duties, and shall severally report to the County Attorney the state of their work and any special matter pertaining thereto whenever required to do so by him.

The County Attorney shall annually, in the month of December of each year, make a full and complete report of the work of his office, and every department thereof, and file the same with the Comptroller of the County, and shall at the close of the term of his office turn over and deliver to the Comptroller, for the use of his successors, the County dockets, together with all documentary evidence pertaining to County business.

COMPTROLLER.

Rule 40—The Comptroller shall keep the books of account, showing the amount appropriated for each specific purpose named in the appropriation resolution, together with the several amounts expended against the same, also an account with each firm or individual furnishing supplies or doing business with the County, except pay-rolls, which may be charged as a whole against the appropriation for each institution.

He shall also keep a claim docket, in which shall be entered all claims properly verified by affidavit. It shall show the date of presentation of each claim, the amount and also the amount allowed by the Comptroller, also the action of the Board thereon and date thereof, *as well as the date of payment.*

All claims shall be audited by the Comptroller before submitting them to the Board. In doubtful cases he shall make a statement of the facts, and may also call upon the legal adviser of the Board for his opinion upon any matter of law, and all such information shall be furnished the Finance Committee or the Board, when called for.

He shall also perform the duties imposed upon him by statute.

COMMITTEE CLERK.

Rule 41—It shall be the duty of the Committee Clerk to keep, in addition to the records provided for in the Standing Rules of the Board, a book properly ruled, so as to show the date of all bills, reports, resolutions, petitions, and all other papers referred to a committee, also a record of all claims, the date, amount and nature of such claim, and what disposition was made thereof.

COUNTY AGENT.

Rule 42—It shall be the duty of the County Agent to grant relief only in case of actual suffering, and to such persons as are legally entitled to public charity, viz.: persons who have been actual residents of Cook County six months prior to becoming dependent on other than their own means for support.

He shall carefully investigate all applications for transportation, and when, in his opinion, transportation should be furnished, he shall report such case to the Committee on Public Service, and act as directed by that Committee.

He shall investigate all applications made to him for admission to the Hospital, the Poor House, or the Detention Hospital for the Insane, ascertain the financial condition of the applicants, and whether or not they have relatives or friends who are by law required to provide for them, and in all doubtful cases shall be governed by the instructions of the Committee on Out-Door Relief.

ENGINEERS.

Rule 43—The engineers of the different County institutions and buildings shall be responsible for the general care and management of the boilers, engines, heating apparatus and machinery. They shall see to it that everything in their department is kept in perfect order.

The Chief Engineer at the Poor House and Insane Asylum shall have entire charge of the water system at the institutions. Also once in every month, and whenever so ordered by the Committee in charge, or by the General Superintendent, he shall operate the force pumps in throwing water on the outside of the buildings, and also see that the hose and pipes inside the buildings are at all times in good condition, and ready for instant service. He shall follow the directions of the General Superintendent in supplying the proper degree of heat in the different rooms, and must give his personal, undivided attention to the duties of his position.

In case of fire the engineers must remain in charge of the pumps; and the Superintendent shall direct and control the action of a force of firemen, which he is hereby directed to organize from employes of institution.

In an emergency, each engineer shall hold himself in readiness to render all the assistance in his power to any other institution, whenever so directed by the Superintendent of the institution to which he is attached.

The several engineers shall be subject to and under the control of the head of the department in which they are employed.

RULE 44—RULES FOR ADMISSION OF CHILDREN AND THEIR GOVERNMENT AT THE DETENTION HOSPITAL.

1. Age. No child under seven (7) years of age, nor more than fourteen (14) years of age shall be admitted.

2. No child shall be admitted who is suffering from any contagious or infectious disease, nor any child who has recently been exposed to any contagious or infectious disease, the County Physician or his assistants being the judges in all such cases.

3. No child shall be admitted to the Children's Ward of said Detention Hospital until the person or persons making the application for admission of said child has made a thorough investigation of the case (and written a complete history on the blank form printed for that purpose), and filed the necessary petition, under oath, setting forth that the child is dependent on charity and eligible to one of the Industrial Training Schools, in accordance with Section 322, Paragraph 3 and Section 3, Chapter 68A, of Revised Statutes, 1889, Hurd's edition:

322. "Petition to Establish Dependency Parties. Paragraph 3. Any responsible person, a resident of any county in this State, may petition the County Court, or any Court of Record in said County, to inquire into the alleged dependency of any boy or girl then within the County, and every boy or girl who shall come within the following description shall be considered a dependent boy or girl, viz.: Every boy or girl who frequents any street, alley or other place for the purpose of begging or receiving alms; every boy or girl who shall have no permanent place of abode, proper parental care or guardianship; every boy or girl who shall not have sufficient means of subsistence, or who from any other cause shall be a wanderer through streets and alleys or other public places; and every boy or girl who shall live with, or frequent the company of, or consort with, reputed thieves or other vicious persons. The petitioner shall also state the name of the father and mother of the boy or girl, if living and if known, or if either be dead, the name of the survivor if known; and if neither the father nor mother of the boy or girl be living or to be found in the County, or their names to be ascertained, then the name of the guardian, if there be one. If there be a parent living, whose name can be ascertained, or a guardian, the petition shall set forth not only the dependency of the boy or girl, but shall also show either that the parents or parent or guardian are or is not fit persons or person to have the custody of such boy or girl, or that if fit, the father, mother or guardian consents or consent to the boy or girl being found dependent. Such petition shall be verified by oath upon the belief of the petitioner, and upon being filed the judge of the court shall have the boy or girl named in the petition brought before him for the purpose of determining the application in said petition contained, and for the hearing of such petition the County Court shall be considered always open."

4. The petition for admission of said child to Children's Ward at the Detention Hospital shall be filed in the office of the County Physician, and shall be considered his warrant for detaining said child until such time as he can, by due process of law, present the child to the County Court, and action be taken by said Court, as set forth in said act.

5. Visiting Days—Visitors to Children's Ward will be admitted on Wednesday and Saturday afternoons only, between the hours of two and four o'clock.

6. Children shall be brought into Court by the attendants of the Children's Ward when so ordered by the County Physician or his assistant.

7. No child shall be detained in said Detention Hospital more than forty-eight hours after having been committed to one of the Industrial Training Schools.

8. Boys or girls arrested by city officers on criminal charges will not be admitted to the Children's Ward.

9. Blank forms of admission must in every case be filled out and accompany warrant of commitment.

DETENTION HOSPITAL.

CHILD'S RECORD.

CHICAGO, ... 189..

Name...... Sex...... Age.... Nationality...... Personal description...... Physician, if seen by one...... . Present state of health........ Where found..... By..... Now staying with..... At..... Father's name...... Father's address...... Circumstances....... Mother's name....... Mother's address..... Circumstances..... Legal guardian..... Address...... Brought into...... Arrested by..... Court record......

10. The abuse of any child by any attendant or employe of said Detention Hospital will be considered just cause for immediate dismissal. Corporal punishment will not be permitted in any case.

11. The attendant in charge of Children's Ward shall enter name, age, etc., of each child and by whom brought to Detention Hospital, in book prepared for such purpose, as soon as possible after the child is admitted, and in no case is any child

to be received until all the rules for admission have been fully complied with.

12. When any boy or girl is rebellious and beyond the control of the attendant, it shall be the duty of said attendant to report the case at once to the County Physician or his assistant, who shall resort to whatever humane means he may deem necessary to enforce discipline.

AMENDMENTS, ETC.

Rule 45—These rules shall not be amended, rescinded, nor added to, except by an affirmative vote of two-thirds of all the members of the Board, after at least one week's notice in writing of the proposed change, to be given in open meeting, and read by the Clerk; nor shall any rule be suspended except by an affirmative vote of two-thirds of all the members of the Board.

RULES OF COOK COUNTY CIVIL SERVICE COMMISSIONERS.

CLASSIFIED SERVICE.

Rule 1—Classification—The following is hereby adopted as the classification of the places of employment in Cook County with reference to examination for appointment under the Civil Service law:

Class A—All positions requiring the applicant or appointee to be a member of any one of the professions; also their principal assistants.

Qualification—No person shall be examined by this Board, or under its direction, for the chief positions in Class A, without first exhibiting to this Board a diploma or license showing such person to be a member of a profession covering the position applied for, or who shall be under 25 years of age or over 60 years of age.

Class B—All bookkeepers, clerical, or positions requiring stenographers, including inspecting clerks, now called visitors, in the County Agents' Department, storekeepers and assistants, and all messengers.

Qualification—No person shall be examined by this Board, or under its direction, in Class B, who shall be under 17 years or over 50 years of age.

Class C—All nurses and attendants.

Qualification—No person shall be examined by this Board, or under its direction, in Class C, who shall be under 21 years of age or over 50 years of age.

Class D—All positions to be filled by persons skilled in any one of the trades, and their assistants, including elevator men.

Qualification—No person shall be examined by this Board, or under its direction, in Class D, without first furnishing to this Board satisfactory proof that he or she has served the proper time necessary to become skilled in the trade covering the position applied for, or who shall be under 21 years of age or over 50 years of age.

Class E—Watchmen, teamsters, hostlers and farm hands.

Qualification—No person shall be examined by this Board, or under its direction, in Class E, who shall be under 21 years or over 55 years of age.

Glass F—All positions of common labor to be filled by males.

Qualification—No person shall be examined by this Board, or under its direction, in class F, who shall be under 21 years or over 50 years of age.

Class G—All positions of domestic work or common labor to be filled by females.

Qualification—No person shall be examined by this Board, or under its direction, in Class G, who shall be under 18 or over 45 years of age.

Rule 2—Sub-Classification.—All approved applications will be entered in the Classification Register provided for by Rule 3, under a Sub-Classification, covering the places of employment to which the position specified in the application blank properly belongs.

Rule 3—Filing Application—All persons desiring to avail themselves of the benefits of the Civil Service Act relating to Cook County and to take the examination under the classified list shall file with the Secretary of this Board an application on one of the blank forms prepared for that purpose.

Blank applications can be procured at Room 205, Court House.

Rule 4—Entry of Applications.—All applications shall be received by the Secretary, and shall be given a consecutive number. When examined and approved by the Board they shall be entered in a register under the proper classification and sub-classification, which shall show the name and address of the applicant, the date of application and the position specified in the application, and no person shall be an applicant for examination in more than one branch of the classified service at the same time.

Rule 5—Date of Filing Application.—No person shall be examined by this Board, or under its direction, whose application is not in proper form and shall not have been filed with the Secretary at least five days prior to the regular examination of the class to which said application belongs.

Rule 6—To Comply with Rules 3, 4 and 5—No person shall be examined by this Board, or under its direction, until Rules 3, 4 and 5 shall have been complied with.

Rule 7—General Qualification of Applicants.—No person shall be examined by this Board, or under its direction, who is not either a native or naturalized American citizen, as required by an Act of the General Assembly of the State of Illinois, approved June 1, 1889, in force July 1, 1889, or are exempt from the operation of said Act by reason of age or sex, or who is not a resident of Cook County, Illinois, or who is under 17 years of age or over 60 years of age, or who has not furnished proper certificates, as to habits and moral character, or who is not in good health.

Rule 8—Examinations. Preserved.—All examinations as far as practicable shall be reduced to writing, and shall be preserved by the Secretary as a part of the records of this Board.

Rule 9—Examinations. Practical.—All examinations shall be practical in their character and shall relate to those matters which will fairly test the relative capacity of the persons examined to discharge the duties of the positions to which they seek to be appointed, and shall include tests of physical qualifications and health, and when appropriate, of manual skill. No questions in any examination shall relate to political or religious opinion or affiliations. The commission shall control all examinations.

Rule 10—Notice of Examinations.—Notice of the time and place and general scope of every examination and the class shall be given by the Commission by publication for two weeks preceding such examination in a daily newspaper of general circulation published in said County, and such notice shall also be posted by said Commissioners in a conspicuous place in their office for two weeks before such examination. The Secretary shall also send a notice to all applicants whose names appear on the register and who are entitled under the class to be examined.

Examinations may be adjourned from time to time by the Board.

Rule 11—Percentage Credit.—In determining the general average standing of each candidate examined, 100 per cent shall be taken as the basis of percentage.

No person examined shall be entered on the Register of Examinations as entitled to appointment, under any classification, who shall not receive from the Board, or from the examiners appointed by the Board, a percentage credit of at least 70.

No person who shall fail at any examination to receive a percentage credit of 70 shall be entitled to participate in any subsequent examination until at least six months shall have elapsed from date of such failure.

Rule 12 — Promotions.—All examinations for promotion shall be competitive among such members of the next lower rank as desire to submit themselves to such examination; and it shall be the duty of the Commission to submit to the appointing power the names of not more than three applicants for each promotion having the highest rating. The method of examination and the rules governing the same and the method of certifying shall be the same as provided for applicants for original appointment.

The Commission will endeavor, as far as practicable, to fill positions by promotion. In all positions in the same general classification, but of a different grade or sub-classification, the position entitled to receive the highest salary will be considered as coming within the meaning of this rule, as well as promotions from one general class to another.

In all examinations for promotions candidates will be given proper credit for experience, ascertained merit and seniority in service.

Rule 13—Certificates to Appointing Power.—All certificates by this Board to the Appointing Power shall be signed by the Chairman and Secretary, and shall contain the name or names of the person or persons appearing on the Register of Examination as having the highest percentage credit in the general classification under the sub-classification covering the position or place of employment necessary to be filled by any appointment.

In cases of promotion the certificate shall contain name or names as prescribed in Rule 16.

In all cases where two or more persons in the same sub-classification upon the Register of Examination have the same percentage credit, and their percentage credit is the highest appearing on said Register in their sub-classification, then the names of all such persons shall be included in such certificate together with their percentage credit mark.

The sex of the person or persons in all certificates shall be governed by the sex specified in the written request of the appointing power.

The period of probation for all appointments shall be thirty days.

Rule 14—Duties of Secretary.—The Secretary shall keep the minutes of its proceedings, preserve all reports made to it, keep a record of all examinations held under its direction and perform such other duties as the commission shall require.

Rule 15—Two Members to Sign.—All requisitions for supplies, or the expenditure of any money, appointments of examiners, and reports and findings of every description shall be signed by at least two members of this Board.

Rule 16—Meetings to be Held.—This Board will hold regular meetings on Wednesdays of each week at 2 o'clock P. M.

It may also hold meetings at such other times as the Chairman may designate.

Rule 17.—Shall be Public.—All meetings and examinations shall be public. All records and documents of this Board shall be open to public inspection and examination by any proper person, at reasonable hours, upon application to any member of the Board.

Resolved, By the Board of Civil Service Commissioners, of Cook County, Illinois, that the foregoing rules be and they are hereby adopted, to take effect and be in force from and after August 1, 1895.

ANNUAL REPORT OF JAMES L. MONAGHAN

Deputy Comptroller of Cook County.

By no means the least important of the County offices, and one from which the most grave and weighty responsibilities are inseparable, is that of Deputy Comptroller, now held by James L. Monaghan. The present incumbent succeeded the present President of the County Board, Hon. Daniel D. Healy, who was concededly the best Deputy Comptroller that Cook County has ever had. The mantle of Deputy Comptroller Healy could not have fallen upon more meritorious shoulders than those of Deputy Comptroller Monaghan, and he has distinguished himself by being an eminently worthy successor of his brilliant and unexcelled predecessor. How worthily he has acquitted himself of the duties devolving upon him is abundantly demonstrated by his able conduct of the affairs of the Comptroller's office since he assumed charge of it. The success of his efforts as a faithful conservator of Cook County's interests has been gratifying and pronounced, and strengthens the general conviction that he is emphatically the right man in the right place. As Deputy County Comptroller, Mr. Monaghan has shown conspicuous ability and a praiseworthy attention to the business of his office. In fine, Mr. Monaghan's administration of this office leaves nothing to be desired in the way of completeness and efficiency. His report as Deputy Comptroller given below will repay a careful study.

LIABILITIES.

BONDS.		
February 1, 1889, 5 per cent Court House Bonds, expire January 1, 1899..	$ 750,000 00	
May 1, 1880, 4½ per cent Refunding Bonds, Series A, expire May 1, 1900..	1,158,500 00	
May 1, 1885, 4 per cent Refunding Bonds, Series B, expire May 1, 1900...	500,000 00	
March 1, 1888, 4 per cent Refunding Bonds, expire $10,000.00 each year, commencing March 1, 1889	130,000 00	
March 1, 1888, 4 per cent Refunding Bonds, expire $40,000.00 each year, commencing March 1, 1889	520,000 00	
May 1, 1892, 1 to 20 year 4 per cent Refunding Bonds, Series C, $67,500.-00 expire each year	1,147,500 00	
OUTSTANDING CLAIMS.		
*Warrants 1885, 1886, 1887, and old claims	166,030 00	
OUTSTANDING CONTRACTS.		
Building Fund, unfinished	58,140 64	
Contingent Fund, unfinished	33,624 60	

ASSETS.

Cash Balance to credit of General Fund, January 1, 1896		$ 37,265 11
Balance to credit of General Fund, account Salary Fund, 1895		775,860 56
Balance to credit of Salary Fund, 1895		30,643 50
Balance to credit of General Fund, account Supply Fund, 1895		609,029 04
Balance to credit of Supply Fund, 1895		11,070 96
Balance to credit of General Fund, account Miscellaneous Fund, 1895		170,014 97
Balance to credit of Miscellaneous Fund, 1895		22,560 03
Balance to credit of General Fund, account Building Fund, 1895		91,859 36
Balance to credit of General Fund, account Contingent Fund, 1895		40,010 44
Balance to credit of Building Fund carried over, 1896		58,140 64
Balance to credit of Contingent Fund carried over, 1896		33,624 60
Balance to credit of Funding Fund, January 1, 1896		13,751 60
Balance		2,569,964 43
	$ 4,463,795 24	$ 4,463,795 24

*Contested claims.

FUNDING FUND.

By receipts from J. L. Monaghan, Deputy Comptroller, and old Interest Fund	$	41,023 20
By balance ending Dec. 31, 1894		27,275 00
Total	$	68,298 20
Amount expended per order County Board		54,546 60
By balance	$	13,751 60

TAVERN LICENSE FUND.

Amount received account tavern licenses during 1895	$	14,304 89
Amount received account tavern licenses during 1894, remaining unpaid		3,033 93
Total	$	17,338 82
Amount paid out from Jan. 1 to Dec. 31, 1895		17,031 32
By balance	$	307 50

GENERAL FUND.

One per cent Tavern License Fund		$ 4,019 50
Gain on taxes, double payments and back taxes		10,619 36
By amount carried from Emergency Fund, 1894	$ 333 40	
By balance ending Dec. 31, 1894	20,158 90	
By amount from 1894 funds	1,771,505 78	
		1,791,998 08
Total		$1,806,636 94
Amount advanced to Salary Fund, 1895	$ 775,860 56	
Amount advanced to Supply Fund, 1895	609,029 04	
Amount advanced to Miscellaneous Fund, 1895	170,014 97	
Amount advanced to Contingent Fund, 1895	40,010 44	
Amount advanced to Building Fund, 1895	91,859 36	
Uncollected taxes, Town and County Collector's Commissions	81,247 88	
Treasurer's Commissions	1,349 58	
		1,769,371 83
By balance		$ 37,265 11

FUNDS, 1895.

SALARY FUND.

From Contingent Fund, July 26, 1895, for Election Commissioners	$	750 06
Appropriation to be realized by tax levy of 1895		805,754 00
Appropriation to be realized from other sources		1,146,176 00
Total		$1,952,680 06

	Borrowed from General Fund.	Other Sources.	Amount Expended.	
Amount expended for jury certificates, election expenses and salaries from January 1 to December 31, 1895	$1,137,948 22	$771,649 77	$1,909,597 99	1,909,597 99
				$ 43,082 07
Deduct loss on amount of actual, less appropriation				12,438 57
By balance				$ 30,643 50

SUPPLY FUND.

Amount appropriated to be realized by tax levy 1895	$ 619,600 00
Amount carried from Supply Fund, 1894, to Supply Fund 1895, account County Superintendent Schools	904 93
Amount carried from Contingent Fund, 1895, to Supply Fund, 1895, account State's Attorney	500 00
Total	$ 621,004 93

	Borrowed from General Fund.	Amount Expended.	
Amount expended from Jan. 1 to Dec. 31, 1895	$609,029 04	$610,126 35	610,126 35
By balance			$ 10,878 58
Amount expended from earnings of County Clerk's Office			192 38
Total			$ 11,070 96

MISCELLANEOUS FUND.

Balance of Road and Bridge Appropriation 1894, carried to Road and Bridge Appropriation 1895, account outstanding contracts			$ 5,455 66
Amount appropriated to be realized by tax levy 1895			191,775 00
Amount carried from Contingent Fund for out-door relief			800 00
Total			$ 198,030 66
	Borrowed from General Fund.	Amount Expended.	
Amount expended from Jan. 1 to Dec. 31, 1895	$170,014 97	$175,470 63	175,470 63
By balance			$ 22,560 03

CONTINGENT FUND.

Amount appropriated to be realized by tax levy 1895	$ 75,685 10
Amount taken from Contingent Fund account Salary and Miscellaneous Funds	2,050 06
	$ 73,635 04
Amount expended from Jan. 1 to Dec. 31, 1895	40,010 44
By balance	$ 33,624 60

PUBLIC BUILDING FUND.

Amount brought forward from Building Fund 1894, account outstanding contracts			$ 36,759 82
Amount appropriated to be realized by tax levy 1895			150,000 00
Total			$ 186,759 82
	Borrowed from General Fund.	Amount Expended.	
Amount expended from Jan. 1 to Dec. 31, 1895	$91,859 36	$128,619 18	128,619 18
By balance			$ 58,140 64

STATEMENT OF APPROPRIATIONS, EXPENDITURES, ETC., A. D. 1895.

INSTITUTION OR OFFICE.	Salary Appropriation.	Salary Expended.	Supplies and Repairs Appropriation.	Supplies and Repairs Expended.
County Hospital and Detention Hospital	$ 96,316 00	$ 96,293 81	$ 155,000 00	$ 154,996 22
Office of Gen. Supt. of Co. Inst. at Dunning	20,692 00	19,940 71		
Insane Asylum	46,500 00	46,280 40	220,000 00	219,970 84
Poor House and County Farmer	24,096 00	23,386 69		
County Agent	25,000 00	24,980 06	100,000 00	99,956 47
Custodian Court House	57,880 00	57,566 98	34,000 00	33,999 84
Custodian Criminal Court	42,600 00	42,088 95	16,000 00	12,575 14
Sheriff	245,800 00	245,259 13	12,000 00	11,998 37
Superintendent Public Service	16,620 00	16,314 80	4,000 00	3,180 69
County Commissioners				
Jury Clerks and County Electrician	52,900 00	52,584 10	6,000 00	5,381 30
Comptroller's Office	14,840 00	14,839 80		
Amount carried from Contingent Fund	....	....	500 00	1,896 49
State's Attorney	41,400 00	41,354 89	1,500 00	
County Attorney	10,900 00	10,093 74	2,600 00	1,535 00
Amount of Balances Carried to County Superintendent Schools' Office from 1894	....	....	904 93	904 93
County Superintendent of Schools	4,900 00	4,899 84	1,500 00	1,369 58
Normal School	25,000 00	24,608 33	10,000 00	8,731 95
Coroner	26,960 00	26,947 31	2,000 00	742 67
Clerk Criminal Court	46,850 00	46,846 44	3,500 00	3,543 06
Amount carried from Contingent Fuud	750 06	7,249 98	....	....
Election Commissioners	6,500 00			
County Clerk and Clerk County Court	201,450 00	201,086 47	12,500 00	12,536 22
County Treasurer	208,490 00	201,504 62	8,000 00	6,246 86
Recorder	179,250 00	175,187 49	10,000 00	8,075 41
Clerk Circuit Court	73,390 00	73,123 75	8,500 00	8,498 89
Clerk Superior Court	59,620 00	59,494 90	8,000 00	6,452 32
Clerk Probate Court	61,976 00	61,252 54	4,500 00	4,499 61
Jurors and Witness Fees and Dieting Jurors Criminal Cases	250,000 00	222,045 64	....	....
Salaries Judges of all Courts of Record	112,000 00	108,705 10	....	....
Treasurer's Commissions	....	5,661 43	....	3,034 49
Total	$1,952,680 06	$1,909,597 99	$ 621,004 93	$ 612,603 55

ESTIMATED AND ACTUAL RECEIPTS OF COUNTY OFFICERS OVER AND ABOVE THEIR OWN SALARIES

INSTITUTION OR OFFICE.	Estimated Receipts.	Actual Receipts Six months, June 1.	Actual Receipts Six months, Dec. 1.	Total Receipts.
County Treasurer	$ 310,000 00	$ 9,969 93	$ 331,526 49	$ 341,496 42
Recorder of Deeds	190,000 00	90,359 15	90,274 55	180,633 70
County Clerk and Clerk County Court	200,000 00	112,090 75	94,885 17	206,975 92
Clerk Probate Court	100,000 00	51,495 55	39,488 62	90,984 17
Clerk Circuit Court	180,000 00	82,950 39	85,863 50	168,813 89
Clerk Superior Court	120,000 00	49,647 00	50,385 00	100,032 00
Sheriff	50,000 00	22,807 86	26,674 76	49,482 62
Clerk Criminal Court	2,000 00	307 65	96 85	404 50
Coroner	1,000 00	475 86	327 80	803 66
Total	$1,153,000 00			$1,139,626 88
Deduct amount held by County Clerk for salaries				5,889 45
Actual				$1,133,737 43

Appropriation	$1,146,176 00
Actual	1,133,737 43
Loss	$ 12,438 57

INSTITUTIONS, TOWNS, ETC.	Appropriation.	Expended.
Dieting prisoners, Jail	$ 50,000 00	$ 42,626 50
Dieting prisoners, House of Correction	18,000 00	18,354 60
For costs, pauper cases, County Court	10,000 00	10,000 00
Humane Society	2,000 00	2,000 00
Telephone Service	2,500 00	2,357 98
State Institutions	25,000 00	21,237 88
Industrial Schools for Boys and Girls:		
St. Mary's Training School for Boys	12,000 00	12,000 00
Illinois School of Agriculture and Manual Training for Boys	12,000 00	12,000 00
Illinois Training School for Girls	11,000 00	6,990 00
Chicago Training School for Girls	10,000 00	9,999 96
Barrington	100 00	43 27
Bloom	200 00	189 19
Bremen	275 00	265 95
Calumet	500 00 800 00	1,298 45
Cicero	1,500 00	1,145 21
Elk Grove	50 00	28 45
Evanston	1,500 00	1,486 62
Hanover	200 00	195 63
Lyons	1,200 00	1,146 75
Lemont	2,800 00	2,695 80
Leyden	400 00	207 00
Maine	300 00 500 00	791 32
New Trier	400 00	274 10
Niles	300 00	98 75
Northfield	250 00	67 90
Norwood Park	100 00	7 75
Orland	150 00	29 60
Palatine	150 00	42 75
Palos	300 00	198 41
Proviso	1,000 00	690 15
Rich	100 00	54 00
Riverside	50 00	15 00
Schaumberg	50 00	23 95
Thornton	1,200 00	1,124 07
Wheeling	200 00	147 65
Worth	500 00	400 06
Roads and Bridges Appropriation 1895 ... $25,000 00		18,907 29

INSTITUTIONS, TOWNS, ETC.		Appropriation.	Expended.
Balance Road and Bridge Appropriation, 1894, brought forward, account outstanding Road and Bridge Contracts	$ 5,455 66		
		$ 30,455 66	$ 5,455 66
Treasurer's commission			872 98
		$198,030 66	$175,470 63
Public Building Purposes, Appropriation 1895	$150,000 00		$ 91,219 47
Amount brought forward from Building Fund, 1894, account of outstanding contracts	36,759 82		
		$186,759 82	36,759 82
Treasurer's commission			872 98
		$186,739 82	$128,619 18
For Election and Contingent expenses, Appropriation 1895...	$ 43,000 00		
For Contingent expenses, 1895	32,685 10		
			39,811 39
Deduction order County Board	$ 75,685 10		
Treaurer's commission	2,050 00		199 05
		$ 73,635 04	
		$ 75,685 10	$ 40,010 04

ANNUAL REPORT OF GEORGE S. OLESON,

County Agent of Cook County.

In his report for 1895, which will be found on another page, the President of the County Board takes occasion to commend the County Agent for the faithful performance of duty, and the compliment is a deserved one. Subjoined is Mr. Oleson's individual report of the County Agent's office under his management, during 1895. Following this is given the County Agent's financial report for the same year.

CASES OF DESTITUTION.

Months.	Married.	Widows.	Deserted.	Widowers.	Single.	Total Relieved.
January	5,587	1,748	401	74	12	7,822
February	7,290	2,068	545	137	26	10,066
March	5,678	1,890	470	122	13	8,173
April	1,257	1,094	294	34	5	2,684
May	608	702	190	16	1	1,517
June	485	591	148	15	2	1,241
July	479	587	129	5	1	1,201
August	424	563	138	10	..	1,135
September ...	411	536	155	9	2	1,113
October	592	659	209	15	2	1,477
November ...	1,106	950	294	12	6	2,368
December ...	2,197	1,300	461	38	13	3,991
Totals	26,096	12,688	3,434	487	83	42,788

NATIVITY OF THE DESTITUTE.

All nations were represented among those who were assisted, as shown by the record below: Americans, 6,124; Bohemians, 3,238; Canadians, 322; Colored Americans, 1,259; Danish, 229; English, 980; French, 504; Germans, 8,673; Hebrews, 2,115; Hollanders, 454; Irish, 6,870; Italians, 2,326; Polish, 6,418; Scandinavians, 2,781; Scotch, 354; Swiss, 45; Welsh, 74, making a total of 42,788.

ARTICLES GIVEN IN RELIEF.

Soap, 47,195 bars; rice, 144,572 pounds; beans, 127,423 pounds; peas, 72,994 pounds; oatmeal, 33,125 pounds; coffee, 19,001 pounds; tea, 15,981 pounds; meats, 175, 486 pounds; flour, 48,300 sacks (24½ pounds to each sack); shoes, 4,018 pairs; coal, 14,785½ tons.

DISPENSARY SERVICE AND SICK CALLS.

The total of visits made by Physicians was 28,889 and 3,210 applications were rejected for various reasons. The following is a correct enumeration of the number of sick calls attended to by the various County Physicians during the year.

West Division	1,825
South Division	678
North Division	221
Total	2,724

HOSPITAL AND OTHER ORDERS.

Number of Hospital orders issued	1,034
Number of orders issued for burial	316
Number of orders issued for Poor House	3,519
Number of orders issued for transportation	111½
Number of old soldiers buried	40
Number of orders issued for medicine	1,058
Number of orders issued for trusses and crutches	14
Number of orders issued for artificial limbs	2

INSANE AND DEPENDENT CHILDREN CASES FOR THE YEAR OF 1895.

Number of petitions filed		1,294
Number discharged	358	
Number decided insane and committed	936	
		1,294

DISTRIBUTED AS FOLLOWS:

Elgin	186	
Kankakee	147	
Jefferson	603	
		936

DEPENDENT CHILDREN.

Number of petitions filed		485
Number discharged	77	
Number found dependent	408	
		485

DISTRIBUTED AS FOLLOWS:

Illinois Training School, Glenwood	157	
St. Mary's, Feehanville	138	
Chicago Industrial School	61	
Illinois Industrial School, Evanston	36	
Home for Juvenile Offenders, Geneva	15	
Home of the Friendless	1	
		408

THE APPROPRIATION.

The appropriation for the County Agent's Office amounted to one hundred thousand dollars ($100,000.00) and was all judiciously expended for relief purposes together with the necessary salary fund of twenty-five thousand dollars ($25,000.00).

A REMARKABLE EXHIBIT.

With the same amount of money as was expended in 1895, 42,788 poor families were taken care of, as against 36,500 taken care of in 1894. Consequently the money relieved 6,288 more poor families in the one year than it did in the other. This speaks volumes for the efficiency of the service.

THE COOK COUNTY HOSPITAL.

The Cook County Hospital is situated about two and one-half miles from the County Court House and occupies thirteen acres of land bounded by Harrison, Polk, Lincoln and Wood Streets. The buildings are numerous, the main or Administration Building faces north on Harrison Street and has five connecting wings, which contain twenty wards. Directly behind the Administration Building

Birdseye View of Cook County Hospital.

is the Amphitheater, or Clinic, and the Engine and Dynamo Houses; located behind these and in rear of main building and detached from same is the Store Room, where all supplies are kept. The Laundry, the Bakery and main Kitchen, the Barn, Carpenter Shop, the Coffin Makers' Shop, the Steam Fitting Shop, the Mattress Makers and the Paint Shops, where the larger part of the necessary repairs for the Hospital are attended to.

EXECUTIVE STAFF.

JAMES H. GRAHAM .... Warden.
M. R. MANDELBAUM .... Chief Clerk.
J. E. McNICHOLS .... Assistant Chief Clerk.
CHARLES LUMP .... Chief Engineer.
JOHN THOREN .... Registrar.
CORNELIUS VANDERPOOL .... Druggist.
E. C. FORTNER .... County Physician.
BROWN F. SWIFT .... Asst. County Physician.

MEDICAL STAFF.

REGULARS.

DR. T. A. DAVIS.
DR. J. B. MURPHY.
DR. CHAS. D. BRADLY.
DR. R. H. BABCOCK.
DR. J. B. HERRICK.
DR. A. R. EDWARDS.
DR. G. F. BUTLER.
DR. A. G. BOUFFLER.
DR. DENSLOW LEWIS.
DR. A. M. CURTIS.
DR. E. L. MOOREHEAD.
DR. R. MELMS.
DR. D. D. BISHOP.
DR. H. C. WORTHINGTON.
DR. E. P. MURDOCK.
DR. W. L. NOBLE.
DR. FENTON B. TURCK.
DR. CHARLES DAVISON.

DR. L. HEKTOEN.	DR. C. E. GREENFIELD.	DR. A. E. HALSTEAD.
DR. A. E. VENN.	DR. C. W. HAWLEY.	DR. J. W. TOPE.
DR. H. J. BURWASH.	DR. A. H. FURGESON.	DR. S. W. BURSON.
DR. A. M. STOUT.	DR. G. SEINN.	DR. F. M'NAMARA.
DR. K. SANBERG.	DR. F. S. HARTMAN.	DR. J. ROSENTHAL.
DR. F. A. M'GREW.	DR. H. A. NORDEN,	DR. LEONARD ST. JOHN.
DR. G. FRITTERER.	DR. R. N. HUFF.	DR. C. FENGER.
DR. C. J. M'INTYRE.	DR. E. D. SMITH.	DR. M. M. LEAHY.
DR. J. A. ROBINSON.	DR. J. E. BEST.	DR. E. H. LEE.

HOMEOPATHIC.

DR. CHARLES ADAMS.	DR. L. D. ROGERS.	DR. F. E. ROBERTS.
DR. E. H. PRATT.	DR. O. F. PIERCE.	DR. R. R. REININGER.
DR. H. R. CHISLETT.	DR. W. G. WILLARD.	DR. W. S. WHITE.
DR. M. B. BLOUKE.	DR. C. H. BEEBE.	DR. C. C. BERNARD.
	DR. J. W. STREETER.	

ECLECTIC.

DR. E. F. BUCKING.	DR. N. A. GRAVES.	DR. W. HIPP.
DR. E. J. FARNUM.	DR. F. E. THORNTON.	DR. JNO. TASCHER.
DR. GEO. M'FATRICK.	DR. H. H. LATIMER.	DR. O. O. BAINES.

THE COOK COUNTY HOSPITAL

Is the institution created by the residents of Cook County, Illinois, for the purpose of caring for the sick in the County who have not the means for securing medical treatment elsewhere. It is under the control, therefore, of the people of the County, who act through the Cook County Commissioners elected by them. The Cook County Commissioners in their turn appoint from their own body a hospital committee upon whom falls the immediate oversight of the affairs of the Hospital. One thousand patients can be cared for comfortably at one time.

EXECUTIVE STAFF.

The executive head is the Warden, who is appointed by the County Commissioners. His term of office is one year.

VISITING MEDICAL STAFF.

The treatment of patients is supervised by a visiting staff of physicians, consisting of three distinct medical boards, each representing the Regular, the Homeopathic, and the Electic Schools of Medicine, respectively. Members are appointed by the County Commissioners for one year, and receive no money compensation. The number of appointments is as follows: Regular School, 38; Homeopathic School, 10; Electic School, 8. This number may be increased in case of need by the boards themselves, and it is customary for the regular-school board to select a number of specialists in different branches to act with them. The physicians so elected are not members of the board. The Regular board meets on the last Thursday of each month, at four o'clock in the afternoon; the Homeopathic board meets on the last secular day of each month.

HOUSE MEDICAL STAFF.

The House Medical Staff (composed of the Internes) is determined by competitive examination, any graduate, male or female, of any medical school in Cook County being eligible. The term of office is eighteen months, and there is no compensation other than board and room furnished at the hospital. The interns are divided as follows: Regular, 16; Homeopathic, 4; Eclectic, 4. The examination for the interneships, which is held during the spring of each year, covers the following subjects: (1) Anatomy, (2) Physiology, (3) Materia Medica and Therapeutics, (4) Chemistry, (5) Gynecology, (6) Obstetrics, (7) Eye, Ear, Nose and Throat, (8) Pathology, (9) Medicine, (10) Surgery. The manner of conducting the Regular examination is determined by a committee appointed by the Board. A second committee, similarly appointed, chooses from the Board three examiners upon each subject, who prepare the questions, and correct the papers without knowing the names of the writers of the papers examined. The examinations for the Homeopathic and Eclectic interneships are similarly conducted.

The interneship service is divided into a Junior, a Middle, and a Senior period of six months each. The Junior period includes three months of service in the surgical and medical wards respectively. The Middle period includes six weeks in the Obstetrical wards, six weeks in the Gynecological, Ophthalmological and Otological, six in the Contagious, and six in the Examining Room and the Dermatological and Laryngological wards. The Senior period includes three months in the surgical and medical wards respectively.

ADMISSION OF PATIENTS.

Any resident of Cook County whose condition demands continuous rest and treatment, and who is unable to pay for medical service elsewhere is admissable. Out-patients (dispensary patients) are not treated at the hospital. The sole judges of admissibility are the examining physicians at the Hospital, composed of members of the house staff. If the condition of a patient is such as to entitle him to Hospital treatment, there is little danger of his being refused admission for any reason, unless it be obviously a case of attempted imposition; and, while the Hospital is intended for the very poor, no emergency case is turned away. Patients are admitted at any time of day or night.

DIVISION OF PATIENTS FOR TREATMENT.

By a strictly enforced system, patients are distributed among the schools of medicine in the Hospital in such manner that the regular school gets a certain nineteen, the Homeopathic a certain six, and the Eclectic a certain five patients in every thirty, the character of the cases falling to each school being wholly a matter of chance. The patient has no option as to the school under which he shall be treated.

EQUALITY OF PATIENTS.

The Hospital facilities are in all cases absolutely free to patients. Under no circumstances are they allowed to pay for service or for special favors. Each patient is on precisely the same footing as every other. The plan of providing especially desirable accommodations in consideration of the payment of special fees is unknown in the Hospital; the most favorable accommodations are used for those who need them most.

PRIVILEGES OF PHYSICIANS.

Physicians have no special privileges. There is no arrangement by which an outside physician may supervise the treatment of particular patients at the Hospital.

EXCLUDED DISEASES.

Chronic diseases, including Syphilis, Pulmonary Tuberculosis, and Insanity, are not treated. Smallpox cases are sent to the smallpox hospital. Contagious diseases are treated in a ward which is absolutely isolated from the rest of the Hospital. On Monday, Wednesday, and Friday, of each week, certain selected chronic cases, as well as partially disabled, or convalescing, patients who do not require nursing, are sent to the County Infirmary at Dunning.

THE NURSES.

The nurses are students of the Illinois Training School for Nurses, and are furnished under contract with that school.

VISITING DAYS.

Wednesdays and Sundays from two to four in the afternoon are the regular visiting days. Visitors may be admitted for special reasons, however, at any time.

THE MORGUE.

The morgue, which is contained in a separate building, in the rear of the Hospital, is open for inspection by the public at all times. It is used for the reception of bodies from the County at large, as well as from the Hospital. Unclaimed bodies are allowed to remain in the morgue at least six weeks and the clothing taken from them is kept longer. Photographs of the unknown dead are taken. A description of lost friends may be filed with the clerk in charge. Burials are made in the County burial grounds at Dunning.

DETENTION HOSPITAL.

Although situated upon the same plot of ground and under the same executive management as the County Hospital, the Detention Hospital is rather an adjunct of the County and State insane asylums. It is the place for the incarceration of patients awaiting trial for admission into an insane asylum, and is in charge of the County Physician, who must reside in the building. Upon the certification of any reputable physician, or upon the filing of a petition from the patient himself or his friends, that he is a proper candidate for an asylum, he may be received at the Hospital to await trial. The Hospital is also the place for the detention and care of dependent children, pending the determination by the court of the person, or institution, which shall be his responsible guardian. Trials are held Thursday mornings, at nine o'clock, before a County Judge and Jury of six men, one of whom must be a physician. Two physicians are appointed by the County Judge to act in the capacity of chairmen of these juries. The County Physician is present as counselor.

CLINICAL INSTRUCTION.

Instruction is given in the amphitheatre in the Hospital building, and students are never allowed to enter the wards. The vast number of patients affords the greatest variety of illustration for the use of clinical instructors. A fee of five dollars per annum is charged under-graduate medical students for the privilege of attending clinical instruction. Women as well as men, are admitted to the amphitheatre.

WARDEN'S YEARLY REPORT.

JANUARY 1, 1895, TO DECEMBER 31, 1895.

HOSPITAL.

Number of patients on hand January 1, 1895		794
Number of patients admitted (January 1 to December 31, 1895)		14,861
Total		15,655
Number of patients discharged (January 1 to December 31, 1895)	13,629	
Number of patients died	1,194	
		14,823
On hand		832
Daily average for the year 1895		808
Infants born during year 1895		360
Infants died during year 1895		64
Applications for admission rejected		1,460
Patients sent to County Infirmary		1,045

DEATHS, BURIALS, ETC.

Number of bodies in Morgue January 1, 1895		14
Number of patients died during 1895	1,194	
Number of infants died during 1895	64	
		1,258
Total deaths		1,272
Buried by County Undertaker	316	
Buried by relatives and friends	767	
Colleges	184	
Bodies remaining in Morgue December 31, 1895	5	
Total burials		1,272

(Of the 1,194 patients who died in 1895, 254 deaths were investigated by the Coroner, leaving 940 deaths from natural causes.)

DETENTION HOSPITAL—INSANE DEPARTMENT.

	Male.	Female.	
Number of patients on hand January 1, 1895	7	2	9
Number of patients admitted January 1 to December 31, 1895	794	504	1,298
Total			1,307

Sent to Institutions as follows:

Jefferson	607	
Elgin	186	
Kankakee	148	
Hospital	15	
Poor House	22	
Died	11	
County Jail	1	
Discharged	298	
		1,288
Balance on hand January 1, 1896		19

DEPENDENT CHILDREN.

	Male.	Female.	
Number on hand January 1, 1895	3	...	3
Number admitted January 1 to December 1, 1895	348	135	483
Total			486

Distributed in the following institutions:

Glenwood	157	
Feehanville	137	
Chicago Industrial School	64	
Evanston	34	
Home of Friendless	1	
Geneva	13	
Working Boys' Home	2	
Home of Good Shepherd	1	
Home for Juvenile Offenders	1	
Hospital	1	
Discharged	71	
		482
Number remaining on hand January 1, 1896		4

COOK COUNTY INSTITUTIONS AT DUNNING.

The Cook County Institutions at Dunning are considered as among the most prominent of the County's many important charges. It is here the Insane Asylum is situated, surrounded by a number of buildings which have been erected from time to time as the necessity for them became apparent. The grounds comprise 257 acres, situated ten miles from the Court House on the Chicago, Milwaukee, & St. Paul and the Chicago & Northwestern Railways. A portion of the grounds is set apart for what is known as the County Farm. The Insane Asylum and detached buildings are finely situated, their general appearance being greatly improved by a somewhat pretentions display of landscape gardening. The farm and its management receives careful consideration at the hands of the officials at Dunning. Potatoes form the chief product, 7,000 bushels being raised during the past year, the entire crop being used by the inmates and attendants at the institution. During 1895 the farm also produced 1,050 bushels of oats, 1,500 bushels of corn, and hay sufficient to feed the eighteen horses employed on the grounds. The farm also produced 60,000 pounds of pork in 1895 as against 13,000 pounds in 1894. As will be seen, the buildings are quite numerous, and may be classified as follows:

THE INSANE ASYLUM.

This comprises the main building which has six wings, surrounded by lakes, ponds, drives and spacious grounds, the grounds affording room in addition for four cottages, a boiler and engine room and a building containing a dance hall.

AUTOPSY HOUSE.

Contiguous to which is a morgue, a green house, a laundry building and barns.

DETACHED BUILDINGS.

Consisting of store rooms, drug store, ice house, paint shop, stables, carriage sheds and tool house.

POOR HOUSE.

Consisting of the main or Administration Building with nine wings and buildings for boiler and engine rooms, ice house, oil storage house and a confinement cottage.

In all there are 246 names on the pay rolls at Dunning, while the institution is run on a per capita cost of 22½ cents per inmate. The official staff is as follows:

THE STAFF AT DUNNING.

GEO. F. MORGAN, Gen'l Supt.
Cook County Institutions, Dunning, Ill.

INSANE ASYLUM.

M. T. CAMPBELL, ... Chief Clerk.
DR. G. W. JOHNSON, ... Chief Male Physician.
DR. ELIZABETH KERNEY, ... Chief Female Physician.
DR. CLARA FERGUSON, ... Assistant Female Physician.
PATRICK QUINN, ... Chief Engineer.
W. C. MITCHELL, ... Storekeeper.
HENRY LINDBLADE, ... Druggist.
GEORGE CADOTTE, ... Supervisor.
MINNIE FENDER, ... Supervisoress.

POOR HOUSE.

R. K. REYNOLDS,..Gen'l Office Clerk and Time Keeper.
DR. J. J. CROWE,..Chief Male Physician.
DR. P. F. CROWLEY,..Assistant Male Physician.
MISS J. OSPRAY,..Chief Female Physician.
JOHN WORDEN,..Supervisor.
OPHELLIA BAKER,..Supervisoress.
FRANK WIMMERSLAGE,..County Farmer.

The following exhibit gives the total number of patients in Cook County Insane Asylum and Poor House at Dunning on the dates specified, with the increase or decrease as the case might be:

Total number of patients in Cook County Insane Asylum and Poor House Jan. 1, 1895	2,948
Total number of patients in Cook County Insane Asylum and Poor House Dec. 31, 1895	2,884
Decrease for 1895	64
Total number of patients in Cook County Insane Asylum Jan. 1, 1895	1,077
Total number of patients in Cook County Insane Asylum Dec. 31, 1895	1,261
Increase for 1895	184
Total number of patients in Cook County Poor House Jan. 1, 1895	1,871
Total number of patients in Cook County Poor House Dec. 31, 1895	1,623
Decrease for 1895	248

The following table shows number of patients admitted, discharged and died at Cook County Insane Asylum and Poor House for the year 1895.

1895.	Admissions.	Discharged Patients.	Deaths.
January	592	316	66
February	510	590	86
March	343	562	70
April	334	545	49
May	392	399	54
June	365	387	51
July	452	308	64
August	369	298	48
September	345	268	42
October	421	243	43
November	486	191	45
December	460	328	44
Total, 1895	5,069	4,435	662

The following table shows number of patients admitted, discharged and died at Cook County Insane Asylum for the year 1895.

1895.	Admissions.	Discharged Patients.	Deaths.
January	64	14	9
February	65	18	16
March	53	25	17
April	36	29	18
May	76	33	15
June	40	35	13
July	93	20	16
August	70	30	14
September	39	15	12
October	61	39	12
November	60	33	11
December	58	43	13
Total, 1895	715	334	166

The following table shows number of patients admitted, discharged and died at Cook County Poor House for year 1895.

1895.	Admissions.	Discharged Patients.	Deaths.
January	528	302	57
February	445	572	70
March	290	537	53
April	298	516	31
May	316	366	39
June	325	352	38
July	359	288	48
August	299	268	34
September	306	253	30
October	360	204	31
November	426	158	34
December	402	285	31
Total, 1895	4,354	4,101	496

A NOTABLE EVENT.

Some of the most horrifying catastrophies which have ever occurred in this country have been caused by the burning of public institutions. The isolated situation of these institutions render them an exceedingly easy prey to flames when once under headway, unless wise discrimination and forethought are exercised in providing ample appliances for meeting such emergencies. How near the County Insane Asylum recently came to being a prey to a terrible conflagration is perhaps known to but few of our citizens. On the night of January 2 last, at 11:40 o'clock, a fire broke out in the laundry, a detached building about two hundred feet to the rear of the Insane Asylum. At the time the wind was blowing at the rate of forty-five miles an hour, and to make matters worse it was intensely cold, the thermometer registering eight degrees below zero. When the alarm was sounded it was learned that the direction of the wind was straight towards the Asylum. The fire company, which is made up of the employes of the various institutions, the chief engineer acting as marshal, was promptly on hand, and lost no time in getting to work. The great Worthington pump, which is a late and invaluable addition to Dunning, was connected with the city mains, and in a short time the fire was completely under control. Superintendent Morgan, in speaking of the occurrence, freely admitted that if it were not for the Worthington Pump and the sufficient water supply furnished by the city water mains, he had no doubt that all of the buildings of the institution would have been destroyed, and that the loss of life from fire and exposure would have been very great. He said that he had been through a number of battles during the civil war, but that not even at Gettysburg did he experience such awful sensations as he did during the comparatively brief time on that terrible night of January 2, when it appeared as though the County Institutions at Dunning would all be destroyed, with the loss of life of scores of helpless human beings which would inevitably follow. To his excited imagination it appeared as though the wind was blowing at the rate of 100 miles an hour, and that the thermometer indicated forty degrees below zero. The Worthington Pump erected at Dunning is one of the latest improved automatic fire patterns, of 150 pounds pressure, throws 1,300 gallons of water per minute, and requires the combined exertions of four men in holding the nozzle when in operation. It is the freely expressed opinion of all connected with the facts in the case that the County officials never made a more timely or more profitable investment than when they purchased the Worthington Pump. Its greatest value is due to the fact that it works like a charm when work is required of it, and that it is always ready for immediate use.

ANNUAL REPORT OF ROBERT S. ILES,

County Attorney of Cook County.

AN IMPORTANT OFFICE.

The duties devolving upon the County Attorney are often onerous and exacting, necessitating cool judgment, much legal erudition with a thorough familiarity with the principles of jurisprudence and the axioms of well grounded legal ratiocination. There must also be unswerving impregnable fidelity in the County Law Department to the interests of the County. These attributes are possessed to an eminently satisfactory degree by County Attorney Iles, who has demonstrated beyond the peradventure of a doubt his capability, proficiency and competency in the office he holds. The report of Mr. Iles for 1895, presented herewith, is pregnant with interest:

SUITS AGAINST COOK COUNTY.

Upon assuming control of the department January 1, 1895, I found pending against Cook County claims and suits as follows:

SUITS.

Plaintiff.	Date Filed.	Nature of Claim.	Amount.
Sokup, use of Seipp Brew. Co.	3-20-89	Assumpsit,	$3,000 00
Sokup and Louis Winsted	9-5-89	"	5,000 00
Sokup, use of Marshall Field & Co.	9-5-89	"	600 00
Van Pelt	3-7-90	"	600 00
Varnell	"	"	5,000 00
H. L. Holland	6-12-90	"	200,000 00
Harley, use of Martin Frank	8-30-90	"	1,500 00
Roth, use of Moses Solomon	11-19-83	"	500 00
N. Barsalaux	3-23-91	"	1,500 00
John Cullen et al.	5-19-91	"	500 00
M. F. Madden	12-3-91	"	7,500 00
Wm. B. White	6-26-91	"	500 00
Leonard	2-1-93	Case	....
M. J. Boland	4-1-93	Assumpsit,	400 00
W. Harley	4-6-93	"	18,000 00
Gerta Subro, admr.	1-9-94	Case	5,000 00
F. Squibb	6-9-94	Assumpsit,	500 00
Jas. M. Purcell	9-5-94	"	2,500 00
S. Penevaire	9-12-94	"	25,000 00
P. Schneberger	12-1-94	"	1,000 50
Baumgarten	3-4-93	"	625 00
B. P. Price	12-21-94	"	1,000 00
M. C. Donahue	"	"	1,000 00
Pillsbury	"	"	1,000 00
Armour Refrigerator Line	8-17-94	Riot claims,	100 00
Alabama & Great Southern	"	"	450 00
Atchison, Topeka & Santa Fe	"	"	791 82
Boston & Albany	"	"	155 30
Baltimore & Ohio	"	"	103 12
Burlington, Cedar Rapids & Great Northern	"		362 98
Central Car Trust Co	8-17-94	Riot Claims,	$600 00
Chicago & Erie	"	"	264 24
Chicago Refrigerator Line	"		1,010 00
Central R. R. Co., of New Jersey	"		1 80
Chicago, Milwaukee & St. Paul	"	"	2,045 76
Chicago, Rock Island & Pacific	"		4,795 25
Chicago & Great Western	"		1,189 14
Chicago & West Michigan	"		521 71
Cincinnati, Hamilton & Dayton	"		153 40
Chicago & Northwestern	"		791 33
Chicago, Burlington & Quincy	"		84,858 63
Chicago, Burlington & Kansas City	"	"	8 82
Chicago Burlington & Northern	"	"	1,101 69
Chesapeake & Ohio	"	"	255 96
Cleveland, Cincinnati, Chicago & St. Louis	"	"	348 61
Detroit, Grand Haven & Milwaukee	"	"	220 00
Delaware, Lackawana & Western	"	"	682 79
Flint & Pere Marquette	"	"	75 00
Great Northern Line	"	"	2,108 23
Grand Trunk Junction	"	"	8,075 61

Plaintiff.	Date Filed.	Nature of Claim.	Amount.
Grand Trunk Ry. of Canada	8-17-94	Riot claims,	$5,494 61
Grand Trunk	"	"	13,103 01
Hannibal & St. Joseph	"	"	480 85
Illinois Central	"	"	431 28
Kansas City, St. Joseph, & Council Bluffs	"	"	979 81
Louisville, New Albany & Chicago	"	"	583 36
Lake Shore & Michigan Southern	"	"	7,088 09
Lake Erie & Western	"	"	1,010 00
Merchants Despatch Transportation	"	"	1,470 91
Michigan Central	"	"	165 94
Michigan Salt Line Car Loan Co.	"	"	5,781 35
Mobile & Ohio	"	"	341 42
New York Central & Hudson River	"	"	1,034 70
NewYork, Chicago & St. Louis	"	"	670 06
Norfolk & Western	"	"	1,382 83
Pittsburgh, Cincinnati & Ohio	"	"	527 23
Pennsylvania R. R.	"	"	1,604 16
Philadelphia & Reading	"	"	169 40
Pittsburg, Ft. Wayne & Chicago	"	"	20 75
Pittsburg & Lake Erie	"	"	182 03
Swift's Refrigerator Line	"	"	300 00
Swift's Refrigerator Transportation	"	"	620 29
St. Louis, Keokuk & Northwestern	"	"	194 83
St. Louis Southwestern	"	"	440 81
Southern Pacific	"	"	344 28
Toledo, St. Louis & Kansas City	8-17-94	Riot claims,	$ 316 07
Union Tank Line	"	"	1,237 95
Union Stock Yards & Transit	"	"	289 61
Wabash	"	"	940 36
Wisconsin Central	"	"	458 14
Chicago & Indiana Coal Co.	"	"	10 00
J. H. Dole & Co.	"	"	2,890 64
Leet & Fritz	"	"	657 00
Peterson Bros. & Co.	"	"	211 23
W. C. Ervin & Co.	"	"	1,227 18
Nash, Wright & Co.	"	"	1,410 97
W. H. Furguson & Co.	"	"	301 54
J. B. Haggin	"	"	2,000 00
John F. Harris & Co.	"	"	3,357 50
Hirsh Hide Co.	"	"	1,851 20
Noble Jones	"	"	448 36
G. Montague & Co.	"	"	458 38
Nebraska Cereal Mills Co.	"	"	594 00
John J. Palmer	"	"	272 80
W. P. Rogers	"	"	638 50
Scribner, Creighton & Co.	"	"	705 65
E. Seckel & Co.	"	"	501 88
C. M. Shroth	"	"	300 00
West, Andress & Co.	"	"	1,939 38
Thos. Wheat	"	"	601 22
Wolff Bros	"	"	219 50
Woodworth & Graham	"	"	801 97
R. L. Burcell	"	"	13 58
M. Gray & Co.	"	"	25 00
J. A. Hutchinson & Co.	"	"	75 30
J. Selby	"	"	238 72
G. Steinmetz	"	"	124 00
Swift & Co.	"	"	13,329 27
J. C. Lineman	"	"	800 00
Total			$476,965 09

All of the above have been disposed of and stricken from the docket, except the following:

Varnell	$ 5,000 00
Sokup, use of Seipp Brewing Co.	3,000 00
Van Pelt	600 00
H. L. Holland	200,000 00
Harley, use of Martin Frank	1,500 00
Roth, use Moses Solomon	500 00
M. F. Madden	7,500 00
Wm. B. White	500 00
Leonard	....
M. J. Boland	400 00
W. Harley	18,000 00
Gerta Subro, Admr	5,000 00
F. Squibb	500 00
Jas. M. Purcell	2,500 00
S. Penevaire	25,000 00
P. Schenberger	1,000 00
B. P. Price	1,000 00
M. C. Donahue	1,000 00
Pillsbury	$ 1,000 00
Chicago, Burlington & Quincy R. R.	84,858 63
Wabash Ry	940 36
Total	$ 359,798 99

SUMMARY.

Total suits and claims, Jan. 1, 1895	$ 476,965 09
Suits and claims disposed of during the year	117,166 10
Pending Dec. 1, 1895	$ 359,798 99
New suits since Jan. 1, 1895:	
April 3, J. L. Bennett, assumpsit	800 00
Nov. 8, Manon Adams, admr. David Adams, deceased, case	5,000 00
Total Law Docketed Dec. 1, 1895	$ 365,598 99

In no case at law has the County been defeated during the year, and in but two cases in chancery have adverse decisions been rendered, and the County has been ready for trial in all cases when reached, and where cases have been continued it has been at the instance of the plaintiffs and not upon motion of the County.

In the matter of the numerous riot claims filed against the County, I secured assistance, as per resolution of the Board, and made a thorough investigation and have a complete record upon each and every claim, and am fully prepared for trial, and the only riot claims now pending are the suits of C., B. & Q. and the Wabash Rys.

COUNTY OF COOK VS. CITY OF CHICAGO.

There is now pending in the Circuit Court of Cook County, the suit of the County of Cook vs. the City of Chicago, which is an action in ejectment to recover possession of the premises occupied by the City for a City Hall, otherwise known as the west half of block 39 of the original City of Chicago.

The suit was entered in the Circuit Court of Cook County, March 14, 1894, and on notice to the City was placed on the short cause calendar of said court April 27, 1894.

On May 22, 1894, the City filed a bill against the County, praying a perpetual injunction against the County restraining the prosecution of the said ejectment suit, to which bill a general demurrer was filed on July 7, 1894, and upon hearing the demurrer was overruled and a decree of perpetual injunction entered July 14, 1894. On Dec. 10, 1894, a writ of error was issued out of the Supreme Court at Ottawa, and on Jan. 1, 1895, I found the matter pending in the Supreme Court to be heard at the March term thereof at Ottawa, Illinois.

I forthwith prepared the case for hearing and filed the brief and abstract, in the preparation of which Mr. Edward M. Harris assisted, and the case was taken by the court on March 20, 1895, and at the October term, 1895, the court returned an opinion, reversing the decree of the Circuit Court, remanding the cause and ordering the injunction dismissed, and upon filing the mandate from the Supreme Court, the suit was dismissed accordingly. The original ejectment suit is now pending ready to be heard upon the short cause calendar of the Circuit Court, and will be heard as soon as reached.

The decision of the Supreme Court is a signal victory for the County, and while it does not end the litigation, opens the way for its speedy termination, and requires the City of Chicago to stand or fall upon the contract of 1872, and makes the question a purely legal one and sets at rest all questions of equitable rights or estoppel, and I am of the opinion that the ultimate decision will be in favor of the County.

In addition to the above, there is now pending in the Supreme Court at Ottawa, the case of Christ. Dahnke vs. the People, upon a writ of error to the Appellate Court of the First District. This suit was pending in the Appellate Court Jan. 1, 1895. The case was decided adversely to the appellant at the March term of said Appellate Court and was taken to the Supreme Court upon writ of error. The question raised was new and novel, and it is difficult to forecast the final result.

In addition to the above suits, the case of Julia Anderson, alias Julia Weir, against John C. Schubert, Clerk of the Criminal Court of Cook County, deserves some mention (although it is not a County case), for the reason that it affects the fees of the Clerk of the Criminal Court, in which the County is indirectly interested.

This suit was an action on motion of the plaintiff in the Criminal Court to compel the clerk to docket her case (which was an appeal from a fine for violation of a city ordinance), without the payment by her of the docket fee.

The suit was commenced April 14, 1894, and the motion being overruled in the Criminal Court, an appeal was taken to the Appellate Court of the First District, where the finding of the Criminal Court was sustained. The case was thereupon appealed by the plaintiff to the Supreme Court of the Central Grand Division and heard at the January term, 1895, and at the October term, 1895, an opinion was handed down reversing the decision of the Appellate Court.

The result of the decision is to deprive the Clerk of the Criminal Court of a large portion of his fees, unless they can be collected from the bondsmen of the appellants in case of conviction, and will materially reduce the revenues of his office, for the reason that a large number of appeals are taken from the findings of police justices of the City of Chicago.

I have recommended to the Clerk of the Criminal Court as a partial remedy, that in each instance where a conviction is had or where a suit is dismissed at the appellant's cost, he should apply forthwith for an execution for his costs and proceed at once against the bondsmen, and have tendered the services of the County Law Department to that end, and have consulted with the City Law Department to secure its co-operation in requiring good bonds and enforcing the collection of costs.

CHANCERY DOCKET.

To this docket are assigned all cases relative to taxes, which during the year has required a large amount of work, and the results have been satisfactory.

From January 1 to July 1 the department was in charge of Assistant County Attorney Edward H. Morris, who represented the County in an able manner and tried several hardly contested cases. His report is herewith submitted.

From July 1 to September 1 no assistant was provided, during which time judgment for delinquent real estate taxes were taken, and a remarkably large number of objections were filed thereto, all of which were contested by the County Attorney in person.

On September 15 Mr. Wm. F. Carroll was temporarily engaged to defend the numerous chancery suits pending, and rendered most efficient service until December 1, at which time Mr. Frank L. Shepard was assigned to the department under the Civil Service rules, and is now in charge and is prosecuting the work with vigor.

In addition to defending against injunction proceedings, we have represented the County Treasurer in all matters for the collection of taxes and in applications for judgment of delinquent taxes, and have outlined a mode of procedure for the collection of taxes, which I am confident will result in the collection of a large amount usually uncollected. In the matter of objections filed in the County Court on application for judgment for general taxes strict proof was required in every case, and as a result the majority of the objections were overruled and the taxes collected, amounting to a very large sum.

At the suggestion of the Honorable C. C. Kohlsaat, Judge of the Probate Court, I made a careful examination of the records of the Probate Court for the purpose of ascertaining the number of cases of escheat shown by the records of the Clerk's office and have a large amount of data upon that subject and there are now pending two estates, in which the County Attorney has entered his appearance.

The case of Catherine Glasser, in which about $20,000 is in the hands of the Public Administrator awaiting to be distributed, and in which to date no proof of heirship has been made; also the case of Alexina C. Toon vs. Cook County et al., which is a bill for partition, in which it is claimed that a portion of the real estate has escheated to the County.

For further particulars in regard to the suits in chancery disposed of during the year and the matters still pending, I respectfully refer you to the report of Assistant County Attorney Frank L. Shepard, which is submitted herewith.

DEPENDENT DEPARTMENT.

This is an important department, inasmuch as it deals directly with persons who would become County charges unless assisted by their relatives. They are principally women and children, or aged and decrepit persons. The work is very perplexing and requires the exercise of great patience and discretion on the part of the attorney in charge, for many of the complaints are without just cause, but all who come must be patiently heard, and every worthy case relieved where relatives within the prescribed degree of consanguinity can be found, who are able to support them.

In a very large majority of cases, this is brought about by agreement without resort to the court, but in incorrigible cases suit is entered, and a trial had, and the parties compelled to abide by the decision of the court.

During the year 110 support cases were tried, sixteen of which were dismissed, and seventeen are still pending, and some 500 cases have been provided for by agreement. In the prosecution of the work, from twenty-five to fifty persons are interviewed each day, and a goodly number of the persons against whom orders are entered have to be brought into court on attachment, to enforce payment. Hence, taken all in all, this is a very hard worked department.

In the beginning of the year, it was under the charge of Mr. Wm. F. Struckmann, together with the "quasi-criminal business," and "insane cases and dependent children," but owing to the volume of business I deemed it expedient to divide the work and form a separate department for support cases, which I did, and placed it in charge of Mr. R. A. L. Dick, who managed it alone until about July 20, at which time I assigned Mr. Herbert Wright to assist him, and on October 18 I relieved Mr. Dick and placed Mr. Wright in charge, who conducted the work in a highly satisfactory manner, until December 1, at which time he was relieved, and Mr. Wm. H. Ward assigned to the position under the Civil Service rules.

QUASI-CRIMINAL AND INSANE CASES AND DEPENDENT CHILDREN.

Mr. Wm. F. Struckmann was assigned to this department January 1, and has been in charge since that date. He has managed it in an able and efficient manner, and has in all instances worked to the best interests of the County. His report is very complete, and I herewith submit it for your consideration.

It will be seen by Mr. Struckman's report that a large portion of his work has been upon quasi-criminal cases that belong strictly to the State's Attorney's office, the County not being directly interested therein. Hence Mr. Struckmann has been serving in two capacities, and has taken his instructions in County matters from the County Attorney and in State cases from the State's Attorney. No conflict of authority has arisen, and none is likely to arise, for the County Attorney clearly understands that he has no jurisdiction in a State case, except upon request of the State's Attorney, but it does lead to some embarrassment occasionally, inasmuch as it is not generally understood that the County Attorney in such matters acts only upon authority of the State's Attorney.

I therefore desire instructions from your honorable body as to whether the County Attorney shall continue to assume the responsibility of State cases on the quasi-criminal calendar, and would suggest that a conference be had with the State's Attorney.

In the matter of dependent children, I have directed that strict proof be required in each instance, in order that where relatives can be found who are charged by law with their support, that they may be summoned into court to show cause why they should not be required to support them; and the same order also pertains to insane cases.

STATE'S ATTORNEY'S OFFICE.

Pursuant to resolution adopted January 7, 1895, I made a thorough examination of the State's Attorney's office, and with the assistance of an expert accountant made a transcript of that part of the record which shows the fees, fines and forfeitures, and from such examination found that the records in the Criminal

Court and State's Attorney's office agree substantially with the State's Attorney's reports as filed with the County Clerk. Hence, the State's Attorney's reports may be taken as a basis from which to compute the amounts collected upon fines, penalties and forfeitures as well as the amount of fees charged by the State's Attorney.

I also found that a very large sum in number and amount of fines and forfeitures had been suspended or reduced, but was unable to ascertain from the record the reason why such reductions were made or fines suspended. The record in most instances being simply: "Upon motion of the State's Attorney, etc."

STATE'S ATTORNEY'S REPORTS.

Upon March 28, 1895, I submitted a partial report giving a summary of the recapitulation of the State's Attorney's reports from December 5, 1892, to February 28, 1895, which shows the amounts collected by the State's Attorney and the disposition made of the same, from which it appears that the State's Attorney has shown and claims in each report a balance due him in excess of all amounts collected, as follows:

Balance as per report, Feb. 28, 1893	$ 18 50
" " " March 1, 1894	7,128 76
" " " Feb. 28, 1895	11,245 86

The following is a summary of the judgments and fines as shown by his reports to Feb. 28, 1895:

Judgments on forfeitures		$ 308,805 00
Fines imposed		32,362 93
		$ 341,167 93
Fines collected	$ 23,508 93	
Forfeitures collected	15,355 11	
Fines uncollected	8,854 00	
Forfeitures uncollected	293,449 89	
		341,167 93

Receipts and expenses of State's Attorney's office, from December 5, 1892, to February 28, 1895:

RECEIPTS.

Dec., 1892, from County appropriation		$ 2,114 06
Dec. 1, 1892, from State appropriation		33 33
Jan. 1, 1893, from County appropriation to		37,060 48
Dec. 31, 1893, from State appropriation		400 00
Jan. 1, 1894, from County appropriation to		41,369 75
Dec. 1, 1894, from State appropriation		400 00
Jan., 1895, from County appropriation, estimated		7,225 81
Feb., 1895, from State appropriation, one-sixth of year		66 67
Dec. 5, 1892, to Feb. 28, 1895, from fines, forfeitures, etc., collected		40,204 04
		$ 128,874 14

EXPENDITURES.

State's Attorney's salary, 27 months	$ 15,750 00	
State's Attorney's assistants and expenses of office	72,920 10	
		88,670 10
Balance of receipts over expenditures		$ 40,204 04

State's Attorney's individual account, including salary:

Salary, 27 months	$ 15,750 00	
Fees due, as per report	47,429 50	
Commissions as per report	4,020 40	
		$ 67,199 90
To salary paid	$ 15,750 00	
To cash collected	40,204 04	
		55,954 04
Balance due February 28, 1895	$ 11,245 86	

The State's Attorney has filed no additional report with the County Clerk since February 28, 1895, and as my investigation closed March 28, I have no means of knowing the state of his office since that date.

From the above synopsis it will be seen that the State's Attorney interprets the law allowing fees to him as providing personal compensation in addition to his salary; in which interpretation I do not concur, but am of the opinion that under the law the fees should be applied in the payment of the expenses of his office aside from his own salary, and that within the intent of the law the salary of $7,000 per year provided is all the personal compensation to which he is entitled, and that if the spirit of the law were observed the County appropriation for the support of the State's Attorney's office would be much smaller than at present required.

NEED OF REVISION.

I am further of the opinion that the law relating to the State's Attorney's office and the Criminal Court of Cook County should be revised and amended, so that no misunderstanding could possibly arise as to the application of fees, and that all forfeitures, fines and penalties to be made payable to the County Treasurer, and by him distributed to the persons or funds entitled thereto. And that it be expressly provided, that the sum allowed the State's Attorney for salary be his only compensation, except that he be allowed a commission of 10 per cent for the collection of fines and forfeitures. Further, that no fine or forfeiture should be remitted or set aside, except upon affidavit showing the facts upon which the motion to suspend, remit or set aside is based; and that the fees now allowed the State's Attorney be made payable to the Clerk of the Criminal Court, and be accounted for by him as other fees; and that the number of assistants required by the State's Attorney be determined by the Judges of the Courts in the same manner as the assistants of County officials are now determined; and that the proceeds from fees, fines and forfeitures be applied to the support of the State's Attorney's office and the office of the Clerk of the Criminal Court, and that any balance and residue remaining thereafter be paid to the County Superintendent of Public Instruction for the use of the public schools.

MEASURES OF ECONOMY.

Public economy requires that every office, in so far as is possible, should be self-sustaining, and I think it nothing more than right that the criminal classes should pay the expense of criminal prosecution, and to that end would suggest that some specific remedy should be provided to meet the evil arising from insufficient and worthless bonds in criminal cases.

The above suggestions are made in response to the terms of the resolution ordering the investigation of the State's Attorney's office, and agreeable thereto I prepared several bills embodying the above suggestions, which bills were duly submitted to the Legislature at its last session. The necessity for legislation is apparent from the fact that the present law was enacted before the volume of business in Cook County had reached its present magnitude, and in its express terms does not meet the present necessities of Cook County. And the present practice in the State's Attorney's office is based upon custom and the judgment of the State's Attorney rather than upon any statutory provision.

SWAMP LANDS.

At the request of the Judiciary Committee I investigated the matter of swamp lands belonging to Cook County, and cash indemnity for swamp lands due from the United States government to Cook County, and have a complete transcript of the swamp land selections located in Cook County as originally selected, together with subsequent selections made by I. R. Hitt, State Agent, and have made a detailed report to the said Committee, together with the recommendation that in order to ascertain the exact status of the case, it will be necessary to have certified copies of the proceedings and orders entered in the General Land Office at Washington, D. C., relative to the swamp lands in Cook County and the cash indemnity due; and am of the opinion that but little can be realized under the Swamp Land Act until Congress shall have enacted additional legislation in relation thereto.

In addition to the work above enumerated, I have from time to time rendered opinions upon various matters submitted to me by your honorable body, and the President, and the several committees thereof, and have advised with and counseled the County Treasurer, County Clerk, Superintendent of Schools, and the Clerk of the Criminal Court, and, agreeable to the order of the Board, have systemized the work in the County Law Department, and have the honor to report that each and every department thereof is in good condition and the work in the office completed up to date.

In conclusion, permit me to tender to your honorable body, to the President of the Board, to the several County officials, and the assistants in my department, my sincere thanks for the uniform kindness and ready assistance that has been accorded me in the discharge of my official duties.

SUPPLEMENTARY REPORT OF ASSISTANT COUNTY ATTORNEY.

CHICAGO, July 2, 1895.

ROBERT S. ILES, ESQ., County Attorney:

DEAR SIR—From January 1, 1895, to date I have disposed of eight (8) cases from the assignments to me. Six new cases have been begun during that time. There are now pending in the Circuit Court, chancery side, fourteen cases; law, one. The case in the U. S. Court has been disposed of.

Thus far the County has not been defeated in any one of the cases or motions where I have had the honor to represent its interest.

To the County Treasurer I have caused to be paid, in compliance with the orders or decrees of the courts, for taxes, the sum of $2,428.32.

You will find proper entries in the docket showing the status of all the cases.

Permit me to return to you my kindest thanks for your uniformly courteous treatment during my official connection with your department.

CHANCERY CASES DISPOSED OF SINCE JANUARY 1, 1895.

Annie C. Wieland vs. Henry Wulff et al. — Circuit Court, No. B. R. 709.

Bill filed Sept. 21, 1891, to establish title and cancel tax certificates of taxes amounting to $236.40. Bill dismissed without prejudice, July 11, 1895.

Wm. R. Alling vs. Giles Bros. et al. — U. S. Circuit Court, No. 22,849.

Receivership.

Petition filed for payment of $835.31 taxes April 26, 1894.

Decree entered by Judge Grosscup for payment of $835.31 taxes, March 11.

Taxes paid to County Treasurer, June 27, 1895.

Jos. T. Ryerson & Son vs. Chicago Iron Works. — Superior Court, No. 151,794.

Receivership.

Petition filed for payment of $294.78 taxes, June 15, 1894.

Decree entered for payment of $294.78 taxes, Feb. 25, 1895. Taxes paid.

Cavaroc Wine Co. vs. Chas. Kern, Co. Treas. — Circuit Court, No. 133,292.

Bill filed to restrain collection of $1,835.31 taxes, and injunction granted Aug. 27, 1894. Bill dismissed for want of equity, May 27, 1895.

Annie B. Hughes vs. Henry Wulff, Co. Clerk. — Superior Court, No. 160,587.

Bill filed to set aside tax title on special assessments, Sept. 4, 1894. Suit dismissed, Sept. 4, 1895.

Annie B. Hughes vs. Henry Wulff, Co. Clerk. — Circuit Court, No. 135,775.

Bill filed to restrain extension of tax rolls for special assessments. Bill dismissed, March 8, 1895.

Au Bon Marche vs. D. H. Kochersperger. — Circuit Court, No. 137,793.

Bill filed to restrain collection of $991.73 taxes, Dec. 22, 1894. Bill dismissed, June 3, 1895.

Taxes amounting to $991.73 paid June 21, 1895.

Henry S. Jeffrey vs. The Cory Car & M. Co. — Circuit Court, No. 127,912.

Receivership.

Petition filed for payment of $222.92 taxes, April 6, 1895.

Taxes amounting to $222.92 paid Nov. 26, 1895.

C. A. Paltzer Lumber Co. vs. D. H. Kochersperger. } Circuit Court, No. 140,723.

Bill filed to restrain collection of $545.58 taxes, March 16, 1895.

Decree entered, ordering payment of taxes, June 17, 1895.

Taxes amounting to $545.58 paid June 17, 1895.

International Gas & Fuel Co. vs. M. W. Honan, C'l'r. & Co. Treas. } Circuit Court, No. 138,694.

Bill filed to restrain collection of tax on capital stock by State Board of Equalization.

Decree entered that plaintiff is a manufacturing company, and by law assessments should be made by local assessor.

People ex rel Gore vs. Mississippi Valley H. & L. Co. } Circuit Court, No. 131,189.

Receivership.

Petition filed for payment of $19.86 taxes.

Taxes amounting to $19.86 paid by receiver, Nov. 22, 1895.

D. H. Kochersperger vs. Chicago Title & Trust Co., R'ceiv'r of Harv'rd Transit Co. } Circuit Court.

Petition filed for payment of $500.00 personal property tax, and tax on franchise.

Taxes amounting to $500.00 paid Nov. 30, 1895.

In matter of the assignment of the Scoville Iron Works. } County Court, No. 12,457.

Petition filed for payment of $158.40 taxes, Sept. 4, 1895.

Taxes amounting to $158.40 paid Dec. 2, 1895.

In the matter of the assignment of the Ristow Potter Mfg. Co. } County Court, No. 13,616.

Petition filed for payment of $136.90 taxes.

Taxes amounting to $136.90 paid Dec. 2, 1895.

W. I. Maddocks vs. The Franz Gindele P. Co. } Circuit Court, No. 136,497.

Receivership.

Petition filed for payment of $198.52 taxes.

Final order entered on receiver to pay taxes instanter, Dec. 18, 1895.

Taxes amounting to $198.52 paid Dec. 19, 1895.

CHANCERY CASES PENDING.

In the matter of the assignment of Jernberg, Griffen & Co. } County Court, No. 10,870.

Petition filed for payment of $167.08 taxes, June 13, 1894.

Comm'rcial Safety Deposit Co. vs. Chas. Kern, County Treasurer. } Circuit Court, No. 135,025.

Bill filed to restrain collection of $3,064.34 taxes.

Now pending before Judge Hanecy, and set for trial.

Ambrose D. Hayward vs. Philip Knopf, Co. Clerk. } Circuit Court, No. 139,846.

Bill filed to set aside tax deed amounting to $205.86, Feb. 20, 1895.

International Bank vs. Chas. Kern, Co. Treas. } Circuit Court, No. 89,420.

Bill to restrain collection of $795.18 taxes, assessed by State Board on capital stock.

Case noticed for trial.

Alexina C. Toon vs. The County of Cook et al. } Circuit Court, No. 148,259.

Bill for partition of land, under will.

County claims that part of property has escheated to it.

Frederick C. Jewett vs. Philip Knopf, et al. } Superior Court, No. 168,535.

Bill filed to restrain issuing of tax deed of $148.50, August, 1895.

T. H. Foster vs. M. W. Honan, Collector. } Circuit Court, No. 140,317.

Bill filed to restrain Collector from levying for collection of tax of $396.80, March 5, 1895.

American Ex. Nat. Bank vs. Chas. P. Newberry, et al. } Circuit Court, No. 95,343.

Receivership.

Petition filed for payment of $491.29 taxes, April 8, 1895.

Now pending in Appellate Court.

Stephen V. Southall vs. Henry Wulff, Co. Clerk. } Circuit Court, No. 107,546.

Bill filed to restrain clerk from issuing tax deed for taxes amounting to $81.36. Money for taxes paid to County and being held subject to disposition of suit.

Marguerite M. Keefe vs. Philip Knopf, et al. } Superior Court, No. 169,152.

Bill filed to restrain clerk from issuing tax deed on taxes amounting to $48.95, Sept. 25, 1895.

Harry R. Mason vs. Mason Air Brake & Signal Co. } Circuit Court, No. 144,545.

Receivership.

Petition filed for payment by receiver of $165.82.

Sidney A. Kent vs. D. H. Kochersperger. } Circuit Court, No. 148,033.

Bill filed to restrain collection of taxes amounting to $2,744.00, Oct. 2, 1095.

Vienna Bakery Co. vs. County of Cook, et al. } Circuit Court, No. 150,139.

Creditor's bill, commenced Nov. 25. 1895.

In matter of Estate of Granville S. Ingraham. } Probate Court.

Claim filed for payment of $396.73 taxes.

As per the above statement, the County of Cook has collected in cash during the present year $3,358.42, $493.82 of which has been collected during the present month of December in taxes, which would have been lost to the County but for the successful litigation in the above cases. The County has also been successful in contesting bills for injunction to prevent it from issuing tax deeds for taxes amounting to $1,071.71.

The benefit accruing to the County by the successful termination of a suit involving the payment of taxes is not to be measured alone by the amount involved in that suit. The County's success in a suit deters many from undertaking to avoid the payment of taxes by litigation: whereas, the County's failure in a suit in which it is made a party defendant, or its delay in cases in which it appears as complainant, would lead a host of people to believe that by delay and litigation they might avoid the payment of their just taxes.

The cases now pending are being pushed to trial and a final disposition as rapidly as possible.

My association with you, Mr. Iles, as your first assistant, is to me an honor, and in the discharge of the duties of my department I take great pleasure and satisfaction.

SUPPORT.

Early in the year I was directed to turn over the Support Department to Mr. R. A. L. Dick, and since then, with the exception of the month of November and part of October, have not given that branch any attention. I desire to state, however, that the work required there is, to say the least, not of a pleasant kind. It has been my experience that almost all of the cases brought for support involve family quarrels, and are frequently of such nature that it is hard to decide where justice lies. Some cases are spite work and persecutions, always brought by wives with the intent of worrying their husbands, and it not infrequently happens that they boast that their husbands will be forced to jail. The Support Department is too often used as a dumping ground for collecting agencies and so-called protective associations, for cases in which they find no pecuniary inducements. The work done is necessarily largely of such a nature that no record can be kept thereof and report made. The few cases that are taken to the County Court represent but a small part of the work actually done. Husbands and wives are brought together and their difficulties settled, and children have been persuaded to provide for the aged parents without taking the matter into court.

INSANE CASES AND DEPENDENT CHILDREN.

In the insane and dependent cases it has been my aim to compel payment of cost and maintenance whenever it was possible. In this regard the Judge of the County Court is the sole arbitrator, and he has been largely guided by the report of the County Agent. The County Clerk, by law, is directed to keep a separate docket of these cases, and no record has ever been kept in our office. The money collected is always paid directly to the County Clerk and Sheriff, who account for the same to the County Board. Since the rule adopted by the County Board prohibiting attendants to transfer paid patients the receipts have largely increased, and the Insane Court is nearly, if not quite, self-sustaining.

QUASI-CRIMINAL.

The State's Attorney is responsible for the quasi-criminal calendar in the Criminal Court, but has seen fit to request the County Law Department to take charge of it. He has, however, from time to time, made requests and directions as to the disposition of certain cases, and has tried one, viz: People vs. Eden, No. 11,939 (the barber shop case), himself, which is now pending in the Supreme Court on appeal.

All forfeitures are turned over to him by his direction, and I cannot report as to what disposition has been made of them.

The quasi-criminal calendar is frequently made the agency in bastardy cases, to enforce a settlement or marriage, and it frequently happens that the witnesses cannot be found, or when found, that a settlement or marriage has taken place, in which case the suit must be dismissed for want of prosecution, or on motion of the County. Appeals from Justices are too frequently brought on straw bail, and allowed to be dismissed on general call. It has been my experience that procedendos issued to the Justices are very seldom heard from after they get there. The Justices are very lax in preparing their transcripts and other papers in the cases sent to the Criminal Court, and very few of them pay any attention whatever to the law requiring the names and addresses of witnesses to be returned. Liquor and assault cases generally arise among the poorer class of people, and are settled in some manner pending the appeal. The witnesses move or cannot be found by the Sheriff, and the defendants are generally ready to move for a dismissal. Early in the year I found that witnesses in dramshop cases, even when subpœnaed, refused to come to court. I had attachments issued for such as could be found, with the result that the Liquor Dealers' Association made complaint that the County Law Department was going out of its way in order to prosecute these cases. Since then very few liquor cases have been taken on appeal to the Criminal Court, and when taken there it has been almost impossible to locate the witnesses. In regard to the giving of bonds, I can suggest but one remedy, and that is to change the law so as to require all appeal bonds in appeals from Justices to be approved in the upper courts.

In Wolff vs. Wheeler, at the present term of the Appellate Court, the court sanctioned my action in the court below in dismissing a bastardy case upon payment of costs of court and the tender to the girl, and upon her refusal, the deposit with the clerk to her order, of all that she could recover in case of a favorable verdict and judgment. The case in question had been on trial before Judge Chetlain for two days, and the jury disagreed. The child lived but three days after its birth, and when the case was called for trial again I persuaded the defendant to pay the costs and make the tender and deposit, thinking it useless to waste two days' time in another trial.

Since this decision a similar case arose before Judge Burke, and the complaining witness objected to a dismissal without a trial, but upon the necessary tender being made the Judge dismissed the case.

For some reason, no Judge desires to hear the quasi-criminal calendar, and it is very hard to get one to give it proper attention. During the year there have been four calendars, and I have spent nine weeks in actual jury trials.

In regard to the amount of costs and fines collected, I cannot give an account of the same without an examination of the records of the Clerk's office. Payments are frequently made to the Clerk without my knowledge, but from an examination of my docket, somewhat over $600.00 in costs and fees has been collected during the past year in the cases tried by me.

The following is a synopsis of the work done since January 1, 1895. I desire to state that among the number of cases dismissed on my motion, are twenty-nine against Fred Nibbe, deceased, and among the cases dismissed for want of prosecution are the cases against the Deputy Sheriffs arrested in Lamont on election day in November, 1894.

Bastardy cases dismissed, parties married	13
Bastardy cases dismissed, child dead	1
Bastardy cases dismissed, for want of jurisdiction	1
Bastardy cases dismissed, after verdict of guilty and before judgment, the defendant having died	1
Motions, new trial pending on verdict of guilty	1
Bastardy cases settled without trial	11

Bastardy cases tried and convicted	35
Bastardy cases tried and found not guilty	6
Other cases tried and fines imposed	6
Other cases tried not guilty	2
Total cases dismissed by agreement	25
Total cases dismissed, motion of County Attorney	52
Total cases dismissed for want of prosecution	54
Total cases stricken from docket, with leave to re-instate	13
Total appeals dismissed for want of prosecution	70
Total cases non-suited	3
Total cases dismissed at defendant's cost	2
Total	296

Bonds forfeited	18
Verdict guilty and new trial granted	1
Jury disagreements	2
Appealed to Appellate Court and confirmed	2
Defendants sent to jail in bastardy cases, who served six months	6
Defendants in bastardy cases now in jail on final judgment	2

ANNUAL REPORT OF ORVILLE T. BRIGHT,

County Superintendent of Schools.

In connection with Mr. Bright's financial report the following excerpts from his exhaustive and able biennial report are deemed worthy of reproduction in this permanent form.

BOARDS OF EDUCATION.

Extract from the law in force relative to the formation of Boards of Education:

Sec. 1. Incorporated cities and villages, except such as now have charge and control of free schools by special acts, shall be and remain parts of the school townships in which they are respectfully situated and be subject to the general provisions of the school law, except as otherwise provided in this article.

Sec. 2. In all school districts having a population of not less than one thousand and not over one hundred thousand inhabitants, and not governed by any special act in relation to free schools now in force, there shall be elected, instead of the directors provided by law in other districts, a board of education, to consist of a president of the Board of Education, six members and three additional members for every additional ten thousand inhabitants. Whenever additional members of such Board of Education are to be elected by reason of increased population of such district, such members shall be elected on the third Saturday of April succeeding the ascertaining of such increase by any special or general census, and the notice of such election shall designate the term for which the members are to be elected, so that one-third of the board shall be elected for each year. *Provided*, that in no case shall said Board consist of more than fifteen members.

SCHOOL DISTRICTS.

The districts now controlled by Boards of Education are:

District 1, Township 35, Range 14, Chicago Heights.........	....	....	2,062
District 2, Township 36, Range 14, Harvey..................	162	3,027	3,520
District 6, Township 36, Range 15, Lansing.................	....	....	1,220
District 8, Township 36, Range 14, Dolton..................	1,184	1,438	1,548
District 3, Township 37, Range 11, Lemont..................	5,173	†5,897	9,496
District 7, Township 37, Range 14, Morgan Park.............	*	1,367	1,815
District 1, Township 37, Range 13, Blue Island.............	3,583	4,628	5,802
District 5, Township 38, Range 12, Lyons...................	....	....	1,033
District 6, Township 38, Range 12, La Grange...............	2,345	2,853	3,343
District 1, Township 39, Range 12, Harlem..................	2,077	2,826	3,271
District 5, Township 39, Range 12, Riverside...............	1,130	1,360	1,442
District 7, Township 39, Range 12, Maywood.................	2,385	3,524	4,755
District 8, Township 39, Range 12 River Forest.............	....	....	1,128
District 7, Township 39, Range 13, Morton Park.............	....	....	2,265
District 8, Township 39, Range 13, Clyde...................	....	....	1,977
District 1, Township 39, Range 13, Oak Park................	5,489	5,588	6,906
District 2, Township 39, Range 13, Austin..................	3,929	5,296	7,257
District 2, Township 41, Range 12, Park Ridge..............	1,225	1,513	1,737
District 4, Township 41, Range 12, Desplaines..............	1,330	1,570	1,950
District 1, Township 41, Range 13 and 14, Evanston.........	1,834	9,239	10,559
District 2, Township 41, Range 13 and 14, South Evanston...	3,218	4,195	4,860
District 3, Township 41, Range 14, North Evanston..........	....	....	1,287
District 6, Township 42, Range 10, Palatine................	1,071	1,041	1,125
District 10, Township 42, Range 11, Arlington Heights......	1,280	1,283	1,480
District 2, Township 42, Range 13, Winetka.................	1,078	1,244	1,576
District 4, Township 42, Range 13, Gross Point.............	....	....	1,066
District 5, Township 42, Range 13, Wilmette................	818	1,064	1,457

Niles Center, 1,125; Barrington, 1,141, will elect Boards of Education next April.

*District changed. †Estimated.

FINANCIAL REPORT.

RECEIPTS.

October 1, 1884, on hand	$ 193 28
Received from interest on state fund	16,600 45
Received from interest on county fund	219 00
Received from interest on daily balance	662 91
Received from state tax fund	290,234 32
Received from fines and forfeiture	4,305 80
	$ 312,215 76

DISBURSEMENTS.

Paid township treasurers	$ 304,410 49
Paid salary from commissions	6,088 21
Cash on hand for distribution September 30, 1895	1,717 c6
	$ 312,215 76

SUMMARY.

Total receipts	$ 312,215 76
Total expenditures	312,215 76

COUNTY CLERK'S OFFICE.

A detailed and very interesting report of the business done by the largest office in Cook County.

COUNTY CLERK'S OFFICE.

County Clerk,
Clerk of the County Court,
Clerk of the County Board,
Comptroller. } PHILIP KNOPF.

Chief Deputy County Clerk..ROBERT M. SIMON.
Chief Deputy Clerk of County Court..............................HENRY L. HERTZ.
Deputy Comptroller..JAS. L. MONAGHAN.

The office of the County Clerk is without doubt the most important in Cook County, and it is safe to assert that the duties of the County Clerk of Cook County are the most important and responsible of any public officer in the State of Illinois. The County Clerk in addition to having the management and control of the County Clerk's office, acts as Clerk of the County Court, Clerk of the Board of County Commissioners, and is Comptroller of the County finance affairs.

The working force of these offices number one hundred and sixty-two clerks, of which eight are employed in the Comptroller's office, seventeen in the office of Clerk of the County Court, and one hundred and thirty-four in the office of the County Clerk. The cost of running these offices exceeding $200,000 per annum, and is divided into the following departments: County Clerk's main office, tax extension department, redemption department, marriage license department, vital statistics department, map department, Clerk of County Court department, Comptroller's department.

MAIN OFFICE.

All business of the County Clerk comes to the office from which it is referred to the proper department.

ELECTIONS.

In this office County election matters are attended to, it being the duty of the County Clerk to call all elections, when made necessary by terms expiring, vacancies occurring, etc. He must have notices printed which states time of election, offices to be filled, etc., and have them properly distributed to the persons charged with posting them.

Certificates of nominations by the various political parties are filed and certified to in this department. After all certificates of nomination are filed the official and specimen ballots are here prepared, ordered printed, together with all other county election stationery, and then properly distributed. After the election the returns are here received and the result is here certified to.

All bonds of elective officers must be filed in this office, also all County Justices of the Peace, Police Magistrates and Constables must here qualify for their respective offices by filing their official bonds for approval and taking the oath of office. A record is kept of such bonds and is open to the public.

JURORS.

The names of all persons selected to serve as petit jurors are written upon small cards in this office and placed in the jury box, which is also kept here, from which they are drawn by the clerks of the various courts as required.

CUSTODIAN OF BACK TAX WARRANTS, ETC.

In this office are kept all Assessors' books when returned by the Assessors of the thirty-three towns in this county. All collectors, tax and special assessment warrants after they have been returned by the County Treasurer and all records of property that has been sold for taxes. The space required to properly store these records is enormous. Notwithstanding the fact that the great fire of 1871 destroyed all records in this office they have since that time accumulated so rapidly that the County Clerk has on several occasions been compelled to ask the County Board for more room in which to store them, and while the office at the present time occupies more than three times the space it did in 1865, and occupies more than one-half of an entire floor of the County Court House, it was with great difficulty that space was secured for last two years' records. At this time the new records number about 800 each year.

TAX EXTENSION DEPARTMEMT.

The volume of business done in this department is simply enormous, being probably larger than any public office in the State of Illinois.

Commencing in the month of February of each year they furnish and prepare for the use of each of the various Assessors of the County books in which are copied a list of all lots in their respective towns. This list is made from, and must be compared with, the Collector's warrents of the previous year, so as to get the names of owners and subdivisions that may have been added during the year, after which new subdivisions must be entered, as well as vacations of old subdivisions, street and alley openings, etc. To get some idea of the magnitude of the latter work, it is only necessary to state that in some years 55,000 new descriptions of property have been placed on the Assessors' books.

The number of Assessors' books to be furnished this year is 285, are large volumes which contain about 800,000 descriptions, and must be in the hands of the Assessors not later than May 1 of each year. During the time that the Assessors' books are in the hands of the Assessors, from May to July, the force of this department is greatly reduced, and is employed making documentary records of all evidence on which tax deeds have been issued on property not redeemed from tax sales.

On the return of the two hundred and eighty-odd real estate books and fifty-four personal property books they are footed and cross footed so as to detect any errors that might occur. A tabulated statement of the total assessment is then made and referred to the County Board, who make any changes found necessary by them, returned and are then corrected, and an abstract of same made and transmitted to the State Auditor to be submitted to the Board of Equalization.

The assessment, as made by the various Assessors, is then copied into new books, called Collector's Warrants. These warrants show, first, the names of owners, the legal descriptions of property, with the Assessor's valuation opposite each piece, also the valuation as equalized by the County Board and the State Board of Equalization, then the amounts of taxes under headings which show for which the amounts entered are levied. In this County there are nearly 250 various corporate bodies, such as villages, towns, boards of various kinds, School Directors and other municipal bodies, who have the authority to make appropriations and which is taxed against the people of their respective districts. These are all adjusted in this office, and the total amount of these appropriations last year amounted to $24,000,000, and required 8,750,000 entries in the Collector's Warrants.

After these warrants are completed (December to January) a warrant is issued commanding the various Town Collectors to make the collections as set forth in said books, and are delivered to them upon their filing a bond and giving a receipt for same.

In this department all certificates of sale are written, and last year the number issued was in the vicinity of 75,000, and according to law each of these must be stamped opposite the legal description of the property in the Collector's Warrants for the next year, for which the Clerk receives no fee.

REDEMPTION DEPARTMENT.

This is the unpleasant section of the office, as nearly all persons having business here have some complaint to make about their misfortune in having their property sold for taxes and being forced to pay large rates of interest to redeem same, etc. In addition to that dissatisfied condition of mind, the force allowed to conduct the business of this department is very small (being only seven clerks) and is at times wholly inadequate to carry on the business of the department, in consequence of which the clerks employed in this department come in for a great deal of unjust abuse, while in fact they are the hardest worked force in the service of the County.

SALE OF REAL ESTATE FOR TAXES.

When the taxes on real estate is not paid in July of each year the County Treasurer makes application to the County Court for a judgment against said real estate, and after judgment has been obtained said property is sold for taxes at auction. This sale can be conducted only with the assistance of the County Clerk, whose duty it is to keep a public record of such sales and issue certificates of sale to the purchasers.

REDEMPTION FROM TAX SALE.

Real estate that has been sold as above can be redeemed only through the County Clerk, who receives the amount of taxes and penalties due, issues certificates of redemption, then turns the amount collected over to the purchaser of the real estate sold at the tax sale, less the amount of his redemption fee.

The number of certificates of sale issued last year was in the vicinity of 75,000 and the number of redemptions of real estate from tax sale was 19,792; this means more than 1,600 each month, and taking into consideration the fact that in order to make one redemption a clerk must go through from ten to sixteen books, and sometimes more, this work is simply enormous. An addition to this work this department answers from 3,000 to 5,000 letters each year in reference to property that has been sold for taxes, and in order to prepare an estimate of same, must go through the same labor as making a redemption; notwithstanding the fact that the County Clerk's Office is a fee office, no charge is made for preparing these estimates.

ISSUES DEEDS.

When property that has been sold for taxes has not been redeemed after two years from date of sale, the County Clerk is the only person authorized to issue a deed to said property to the person holding the certificate of sale.

This work is also done in the Redemption Department, and the number of such deeds issued last year was 450.

MARRIAGE LICENSE DEPARTMENT.

Of all the departments in the County Clerk's Office, the one fearing the legend "Marriage Licenses and Naturalization" is probably the one in which the public takes the greatest interest.

The law provides that all persons desiring to have a marriage ceremony performed in Cook County must first obtain a license from the County Clerk.

The business transacted here is yearly assuming greater proportions in due conformity with the growth of the city.

Since the great fire 246,000 licenses have been issued; twenty years ago the number issued each year did not exceed 4,000; since that time there has been a gradual increase, the greatest number issued in one year being 16,500, which occurred "World's Fair Year." Even last year with its financial embarrassment has not in any great degree interfered with the business in this department, the number last year being 15,515.

Record of these licenses has been kept since the fire, and embraces twenty-one large volumes which are kept in a vault alphabetically arranged and have male and female indexes.

NATURALIZATION.

It was not until 1874 that the County Court was authorized to issue naturalization declarations, but since that time the work has grown rapidly and at the present time nearly all Declarations of Intention of persons residing in this County are taken out at this department as this office is considered by most foreigners the only place to apply for their "first papers."

The average number issued each year is now between 2,000 and 3,000; during the year when it became a law that no person could work for the City without first having declared their intentions to become citizens the number reached 8,500. At the present time the County Clerk's vaults contain 80,000 of such registered applicants, comprising twenty-six large volumes.

CERTIFICATES OF MAGISTRACY.

Connected with this same department is still another branch of business that is yearly assuming greater proportions, viz: the verification of notarial signatures to deeds, oaths depositions and so forth; also certificates of magistracy of Justices of the Peace, Police Magistrates, Constables, etc., the County Clerk being the only County official authorized to issue same, his office being the place where all of such officials must register their commissions.

There is a great increase in the number of these officials each year, the number here registered being almost 4,000, and the fact that nearly every State in the Union now requires a County Clerk's certificate under seal to all documents recorded in their respective States, makes it necessary to issue a great number of same, the number last year being 13,095.

VITAL STATISTICS DEPARTMENT.

This department was created in 1877 by an Act of the General Assembly, by virtue of said act creating a State Board of Health, giving said Board complete supervision of the State system of registration of births and deaths, charging them with the duty of prescribing such forms, books, etc., necessary for a registration of vital and mortuary statistics. They also made it the duty of all physicians and accouchers of the State to register their names with the County Clerk of the county in which they reside; also requiring them, under penalty of law, to the County Clerk, within thirty days, all births and deaths which may come under their supervision, upon forms prescribed by the State Board of Health and furnished by the County Clerk.

Since the adoption of this act the County Clerk has kept a register of physicians and accouchers, and at the present time this register shows 6,715 names. He has also kept an official record of all births and all deaths, and is authorized to issue certified copies of returns of births and deaths. All of this work has grown so large that it requires the entire time of two clerks to attend to these duties.

The number of large records now stored in this office, running from 1878 to 1895, are thirty-six of deaths, showing 321,568 deaths; from 1878 to 1895, are thirty-eight of births, showing 392,500 births. The number of deaths in 1895 were almost 30,000; the number of births in 1895 were almost 35,000.

MAP DEPARTMENT.

The Map Department of the County Clerk's office was organized after the great fire of 1871, when all records made previous to that time were destroyed. It then became apparent that this department was necessary, and would be of great value. The loss of all records by fire made it very difficult for this department to organize and obtain the desired maps, as there was only one abstract firm in the city which had copies of these records and were able to furnish the information necessary to construct the maps for this office. But notwithstanding all the obstacles and difficulties that were met, they are now complete, and they show every parcel of land, with their dimensions, in the entire County of Cook; also all railroads, public roads, rivers, canals, and divisions of land; also vacations of all descriptions, openings of streets and alleys (provided they are recorded according to the laws of this State). They also show the boundary lines of all incorporated cities, villages, etc.

This department employs four men, who have charge of these self-constructed maps, being taken only from recorded instruments of every township in Cook County. They are large books, and the principal duties of these clerks are to keep said maps posted with all the latest records in the Recorder's Office, so as to give the various departments in the County Clerk's office any legal information necessary to conduct the work of making assessors' books, collectors' warrants, etc.

This department has been found to be of great value to the public, real-estate dealers, surveyors, etc., as they have free access to these maps, and will here be given any information in reference to same desired. In the year 1895 about 600 new recorded instruments relating to maps had to be copied on tracing paper in the Recorder's office by this department, and afterwards entered in the maps of this office, a list of which also must be furnished to the Tax Department previous to May 1 each year, for the purpose of entering same in the various assessors' books, in order to assist said assessors to make the assessments for general taxes, and no changes can be made in the assessors' rolls without the consent of this department. This department also has charge of the maps of the various school districts in the country towns, where each district levies its own taxes for school purposes, and sends same to the County Clerk to be spread on the collectors' warrants for their respective towns said districts being determined by the maps in this department.

Notwithstanding the fact the County Clerk receives no money from the State or from the County, and also does a great amount of work heretofore mentioned without compensation of any kind, the figures below will show that this office not only is self-sustaining, but manages to turn in a balance each year.

Receipts for 1895.		These Amounts Represent the Following Work Performed for Fees.
For Marriage Licenses	$ 23,272 50	15,515 Marriage Licenses issued.
For Tavern Licenses	117 00	117 Tavern Licenses issued.
For Estrays	2 70	
For recording papers	933 05	2,700 misc. papers recorded.
For Certificates under seal	3,273 80	13,095 certificates issued.
For making copies	353 15	471 copies of papers made.
For searching records	12 00	
For qualifying Justices	86 00	86 Justices' bonds approved, filed, etc.
For declarations of intention	1,103 00	2,206 Declarations of Int. issued.
For issuing Tax Deeds	2,539 10	450 Tax Deeds issued.
For County Court receipts	60,669 42	See report of County Court.
For making Collectors' warrants	78,451 06	*8,500,000 items extended on Collectors' warrants.
For making Assessors' books	14,792 50	750,000 descriptions written and compared in Assessors book.
For entering judgments	6,010 62	305,000 judgments entered.
For attending tax sale and issuing certificates of sale	14,000 00	70,000 certificates of sale issued.
For cancellation certificates of sale	3,347 30	11,000 certificates of sale cancelled in books and filed.
For redemption fees	21,277 58	19,792 redemptions from tax sale made.
Total	$230,240 78	
Receipts for 1894	$220,201 01	
Increase over 1894	$ 10,039 77	

*As neither the State nor County pay the County Clerk for extending their taxes this number exceeds the amount paid for by about 4,000,000 extensions.

CLERK OF THE COUNTY COURT.

The duties of this department are many and varied, the County Court being a court of general and special jurisdiction.

Among the special business of said court may be specified:

The trial of lunatic cases, of which there were 1,141 cases during the past year.

The trial of dependent boys and girls, of which there were 437 cases in the same period.

The trial of deaf, dumb, blind, and feebled minded persons, of which there were 21 cases in same period.

The trial of support cases, of which there were 136 cases, wherein the Clerk of this Court not only performs the usual clerk duties, such as docketing and recording all proceedings and issuing process, but in addition receives and keeps account of all moneys ordered paid, and pays out the same to the parties entitled thereto, all of which necessitates the keeping of a complete set of books and takes up nearly all the time of one clerk, for which no fee can be charged.

The trial of special assessment cases, of which there were 1,283 cases last year, and the clerk in addition to keeping the records of same is charged with the additional duty of certifying the same to the collectors of the various cities, towns, etc.

Judgment on delinquent taxes occupy the attention of the court and clerk during the July term of each year, and very often extends over to the September term of court, as in nearly all cases of objections filed to these judgments an appeal is prayed to the Supreme Court, either by the city or the objector, as the case may be.

In addition to the above are the election records, the County Court having sole jurisdiction of all matters pertaining to elections within the Election Commissioners' district.

The following is a statement of work done in 1895:

Lunatic cases filed	1,141
Dependent girls, cases filed	135
Dependent boys, cases filed	302
Deaf, dumb, blind, and feebled minded, cases filed	21
Pauper support, cases filed	136
Common law cases filed, being assignment appeal and insolvent cases	1,330
Naturalization papers issued	444
Special assessment cases filed	1,283
Objections filed	1,399
Affidavits made	81
Certified copies made	folios, 68,124
Adoption cases filed	13

The above summary shows merely the number of cases filed, etc., during the year, but does not show the actual work done in this office. As a matter of fact, the court has disposed of one law calendar containing 1,304 cases, the same being cases which had heretofore been filed in previous years, in addition to said law calendar. The court has also disposed of all special assessment cases filed during the year 1895, viz: 1,283 cases; also a number of cases continued from the previous year.

The County Court having sole jurisdiction in voluntary assignments, special assessment, insolvent debtors', lunatic, dependent boys' and girls,' support cases and delinquent taxes, and the same being nearly all emergency matters, it is somewhat difficult to make a clear and succinct statement of the amount of work done, as especially in voluntary assignments, the time of the court is sometimes wholly taken up for weeks, and even months, in the disposition of a single case.

Comptroller's department, see Comptrollers' report, page 84.

TOWNS IN COOK COUNTY.

BARRINGTON.	*LAKE VIEW.	PALOS.
BLOOM.	LEMONT.	PROVISO.
BREMEN.	LEYDEN.	RIVERSIDE.
*CALUMET.	LYONS.	RICH.
CICERO.	†MAINE.	SCHAUMBERG.
ELK GROVE.	NEW TRIER.	THORNTON.
†EVANSTON.	NILES.	WHEELING.
HANOVER.	NORTHFIELD.	WORTH.
*HYDE PARK.	†NORWOOD PARK.	*SOUTH CHICAGO.
*JEFFERSON.	ORLAND.	*WEST CHICAGO.
*LAKE.	PALATINE.	*NORTH CHICAGO.

*Towns wholly within the limits of the City of Chicago.
†Partly within the limits of the City of Chicago.
Towns not otherwise specified are wholly outside the city limits.

REPORT OF FRANK J. GAULTER,

Clerk of Circuit Court of Cook County.

JUDGES.

M. F. TULEY, Chief Justice.	O. H. HORTON.
CHARLES G. NEELY.	A. N. WATERMAN.
EDWARD F. DUNNE.	FRANCIS ADAMS.
R. S. TUTHILL.	FRANK BAKER.
R. W. CLIFFORD.	THOMAS G. WINDES.
ELBRIDGE HANECY.	JOHN GIBBONS.
ABNER SMITH.	EDMUND W. BURKE.

Number of suits commenced in 1895, 12,244, which was divided as follows: 4,377 Chancery suits, 9, 907 law suits. There were also filed 68 burnt record suits, 969 mechanics' liens, 1,934 justice transcripts and 2,980 citizens naturalized.

The receipts for the year were $173,870. The net receipts after paying all expenses of the office, were $95,870.47.

The judges of the court disposed of the following cases during the year 1895: 7,969 common law cases, 3,251 chancery cases and 1,598 confessions. Condemnation cases, 400 verdicts.

The cost of filing a suit is $10; the cost of filing condemnation suit is $20; defendants' cost $3; mechanics' liens, $1; justice transcripts, $2; naturalization papers, 50 cents; burnt record suit, $6; defendants' cost, B. R., $2.

The assignment of cases in the Circuit Court is done by the Clerk of the Court, law cases being assigned from one to nine to the Law Judges, and Chancery cases are assigned in rotation, one to each Chancery Judge. The Chief Justice assigns the Judges of the Circuit Court in their turn to hold Criminal Court.

There are fourteen Judges of the Circuit Court assigned as follows: Nine Common Law, four Chancery Law and one Appellate Court.

A general call of the docket of all cases having had their day in Court is held every two years. The next general call in the Circuit Court will be held about May 1, 1896. The Judges of the Circuit Court meet in December of each year and designate the number of employes in the different County Offices; after which the Cook County Commissioners meet and appropriate the salary for the same.

The following are legal holidays: Jan. 1, Feb. 12, Feb. 22, May 30, July 4, Labor Day, Thanksgiving Day and Dec. 25.

REPORT OF STEPHEN D. GRIFFIN,

Clerk of Superior Court, Cook County.

SUITS INSTITUTED AND DISPOSED OF.

During the year nine thousand (9,000) suits were disposed of in the Superior Court, and eight thousand one hundred and twenty-two (8,122) new suits were instituted therein. This showing leaves the calendar of the court not much less crowded than it was in 1894.

PENDING SUITS.

At the close of 1895 numbered eleven thousand (11,000), and eleven hundred (1,100) people were naturalized through the machinery of the court.

THE PROFIT

Accruing to the county is evidenced by the amount paid to the County Treasurer from the Superior Court over and above all expenses, aggregating forty thousand five hundred and thirty-seven dollars ($40,537.00).

JUDGES.

HENRY M. SHEPARD, Chief Justice.

JOSEPH E. GARY.	JONAS HUTCHINSON.
THEODORE BRENTANO.	PHILLIP STEIN.
WILLIAM G. EWING.	JAMES GOGGIN.
JOHN BARTON PAYNE.	HENRY V. FREEMAN.
ARTHUR H. CHETLAIN.	NATHANIEL C. SEARS.

REPORT OF E. J. MAGERSTADT,

Clerk of the Criminal Court.

During the last few years, there being a general stagnation of business, and various other causes may have led to an increase of offenses against the law of a criminal nature, and in consequence the Criminal Courts have been burdened with cases, which naturally increases the work in the Clerk's Office; during the year 1895 there were 3,671 indictments returned by the various Grand Juries, and in addition thereto there were 2,444 "No Bills" which must be entered in a proper manner in the Books at the Clerk's Office, as a matter of Record; the indictments returned are in some instances very voluminous and contain as much as one hundred pages and more, in a few cases there were from fifteen to twenty defendants, and inasmuch as the law requires a copy of each indictment to be made in each and every case, for each and every department before they can be arraigned, such work cannot be allowed to accumulate, and a force of never less than twelve men are constantly at work for this branch of the service.

The various branches of the Criminal Court tried 4,120 cases during the year 1895, of which number 1,710 were convicted of the crime with which they were charged. The number of aquittals, including *nolle prosse* and striking from the docket with leave to reinstate, amounted to 2,410; during the same year there were 1,507 bonds for defendants approved by the Court, which are in addition to an unprecedented large number of bonds sent from Police Magistrates, and exceeded by far any year in the history of Criminal Court proceedings of Cook County, all of which have to be indexed in alphabetical order, and filed, and involving a large amount of clerical labor.

When we further take in consideration that the complete record in over 5,000 cases has been written, under the old style of Common Law form, which is still in use in this State, and which augments the amount of clerical labor, without adding anything to a correct and concise understanding of the case, it is comparatively easy to comprehend the extent and the magnitude of the work accomplished by this office.

It is no exaggeration to state that the office of the Clerk of the Criminal Court of Cook County stands at the present time at the top of all County Offices for efficiency in its staff of Deputies; Mr. Ernest J. Magerstadt, the present Clerk of the Criminal Court has the peculiar faculty of selecting the right man in the right place; in addition thereto he can be congratulated in securing the services of Mr. Wm. C. Lawson for his Chief Deputy; a gentleman who is eminently well qualified to conduct the business at all times, intricate affairs of such an important office to the satisfaction of all concerned, especially to the gentlemen of the legal profession, whose business, or rather the business of their clients, brings them into daily intercourse with the office.

REPORT OF STATE'S ATTORNEY.

Review of the Business Transacted.

The growth of the criminal business of Cook County during the last decade has been commensurate with the growth of the County in other respects. Since 1885 the criminal business of Cook County has increased over 200 per cent. From December 1, 1892, to December 1, 1895, a period of three years, the Grand Jury, under the direction of the State's Attorney, disposed of over six thousand cases more than during any four years in the history of the County.

At the commencement of the administration of Mr. Kern there were fifteen hundred bail cases undisposed of pending before the Grand Jury and upon which indictment had not been found. Such an accumulation of bonds made it necessary for a case to lie in the office of the Clerk of the Criminal Court for nearly a year before it was reached by the Grand Jury. During November, 1895, and at least ten months before that date, there were heard, in addition to the jail cases, every bail case wherein the bond had been filed in the office of the Clerk of the Criminal Court three days prior to their respective adjournments of the Grand Juries.

As a result of having the bail cases heard before the Grand Jury as fast as they are filed in the office of the Clerk of the Criminal Court, the percentage of indictments in bail cases is as great as in that of jail cases. Prior to the administration of Mr. Kern there were indictments in only 5 per cent of the bail cases. During the administration of the present State's Attorney there have been indictments and convictions in 50 per cent of the bail cases. The business of the Criminal Court of Cook County is now up to date. There are practically no bail cases pending untried or uncalled except the indictments of the last Grand Jury.

It has been the policy of this administration to insist that at least 50 per cent of the indictments of any one Grand Jury shall be tried before the assembling of the next Grand Jury. The current year, from January 1, 1895, to January 1, 1896, will show the largest business and the largest percentage of convictions in the history of any county in the United States.

A complete revolution has been made in dealing with the defendants under bail. In former years, prior to 1892, the judgment of the Criminal Court upon a forfeited bail bond was considered a matter of so little importance that the abstract-makers did not note it in their examination of title. The forfeiture of a bail bond meant the complete escape of the person charged with crime. It seemed to the present State's Attorney that no such immunity ought to obtain in a proper administration of the criminal law. That the poor or friendless defendant should not, by reason of his inability to give bail, be subjected to punishment, while the defendant on bail should escape punishment, or trial, by simply forfeiting his bond. Out of the thousands of bail bonds taken in the Criminal Court during the last three years, not over 5 per cent of the persons on bail have failed to appear for trial. Three years ago at this time there were over seven hundred people in jail. Today the number does not exceed four hundred and fifty. Certainty and swiftness of punishment is slowly driving the criminals into other great cities. There is no place on earth where criminal justice is meted out more swiftly than under the present administration in Cook County.

JOSEPH E. GARY .... Presiding Justice.
HENRY M. SHEPARD .... Justice.
ABBA N. WATERMAN .... Justice.

REPORT OF CLERK OF PROBATE COURT.

Financial and Business Report of the Clerk of the Probate Court.

By an act of the Legislature, approved April 27, 1877, as amended by an act approved May 24, and in force July 1, 1881, Probate Courts were established in all counties in the State of Illinois having a population of 70,000 or more.

Thus far the citizens of only two counties, Cook and Peoria, are entitled, by virture of their population, to take advantage of this act. The idea that the Probate Court would be an advantage to the bar and to the people led to its establishment. That it has been an advantage to both, far greater than was expected, there is no question. From the time the functions of the Probate and County Courts were separated, the business of the former has showed a marked and wonderful increase.

The public occasionally sees a newspaper item stating that a certain estate had been admitted to probate, or that the estate of some well-known citizen had been inventoried at a certain sum; but further than this the great populace of Cook County knows little or nothing. Yet the Probate Court transacts more business during the year than the majority of our business houses. Property representing millions of dollars passes through this court every twelve months. The administration of vast estates, great property interests, the education and care of thousands of children, and the supervision of the estates of the drunkard, spendthrift and insane come under its jurisdiction.

To handle this immense volume of business the County Board allows forty-four clerks, as follows: One chief clerk, three assistants to the Judge, one cashier, five record writers, one fee and process clerk and one assistant, one minute clerk, two general clerks, two docket clerks, one claim clerk, one citation clerk and one assistant, one transcript clerk, one comparer, three vault clerks, two stenographers, one grant clerk and sixteen recording clerks.

There is not an unimportant position in the above list. One of the assistants to the Judge is responsible for the approval of all bonds and the accuracy of the proofs of all wills and heirships; another for the value of every estate as shown by the inventory and appraisement and for all matters of real estate, and the third for the closing up of all estates and the approval of final accounts. The latter must see that all claims against estates are paid and that justice is done to all parties in interest. The minute clerk must enter the orders which the Judge makes with absolute correctness. An error would work great hardship and perhaps cause infinite trouble. The docket clerk must be equally accurate. If the vault clerk should place a paper in the wrong file, untold labor would be entailed in its recovery. If the citation clerk sends the Sheriff for a person who is not liable for a citation, he commits a most serious mistake. The claim clerk must see that all claims filed for adjustment in a certain term are on the claim docket at the proper time and that none are on not so filed. The record writer must use the utmost care in order that there may be no flaw in the record, which is of greater importance, if possible, than anything else connected with the office. And so on through the list; every position is responsible; every man knows his duty and does it.

The Probate Court is a court of detail. This is true of any county office, but especially so with this. The process necessary to issue a citation will best illustrate this point. A citation is a writ issued out of the Court requiring a person to appear before the Court and show cause why a certain thing has or has not been done. The citation clerk examines first, the docket to see what estates are liable to citation and makes a list of the same. Second, he goes through the indexes of the estates for the file numbers. Third, gets out the files and examines every paper in each estate to see if there are any papers on file which makes a citation unnecessary. Fourth, writes the writs. Fifth, puts the seal on them. Sixth, enters them in the process docket. Seventh, enters them in the fee book and gets addresses of parties cited. Eighth, enters them in his private record. Ninth, enters them in the minute book. Tenth, enters them in the docket. Eleventh, makes bills of cost and delivers writs to Sheriff. Twelfth, on return day enters Sheriff's fees and takes the writs before the Court. Thirteenth, files the writs. Fourteenth, enters return in process docket. Fifteenth, enters Sheriff's fees in fee book. Sixteenth, writes the record of the whole proceeding. Sixteen different processes, and all the public sees is a piece of paper called a citation. The same rule of detail runs through every department.

At the head of this important branch of our County government is the Clerk of the Court, Abijah O. Cooper. He was elected Nov. 6, 1894, and took charge of the office on Dec. 3 of the same year. He brought to his new position a business experience of twenty years and a record for honesty and integrity in business and as a leader of men that has only been emphasized by his public career thus far. He is a man of energy, education and ability. A close observer, capable of great application and full of resources. He entered upon his new duties as he had entered upon every undertaking in life, with the determination to succeed, and, as in everything else, he has succeeded. Under his able direction and his faculty of discrimination shown in selecting the right man for the right place, he has improved the workings of the entire office. Each department is like a portion of a great machine, every piece having its special work but each depending on the other.

Being a man of action, he made few promises as to what he intended to do, but at the end of his first year in office he has turned over to the Board of County Commissioners the most satisfactory annual statement that ever came from the Probate Court.

The following is a comparative statement of the business of the office during the last year of Mr. Cooper's predecessor and the first year of his own administration. The most significant item in it is that in addition to paying all the expenses of his office he turned over to the County Treasurer $29,731.63, being $12,861.84 more than was turned over by his predecessor the year before.

	1894.	1895.
Earnings from transcripts	$ 3,827 85	$ 4,263 75
Costs released	21,708 02	26,274 97
Gross earnings	126,884 33	136,378 94
Total collections	69,924 39	96,752 44
Total amount paid to County Treasurer	16,869 79	29,731 63
Number of pages of record written	5,985	9,085
Total number of citations issued	1,669	2,641
Letters granted, administration and with will annexed	....	913
Letters of administration granted	....	1,326
Letters of administration *de bonis non* granted	....	119
Letters of guardianship granted	....	579
Letters of conservatorship granted	....	84
Total number of estates	....	3,021
Wills proved and admitted to record	....	884
Decrees for sale of real estate entered	....	259
Miscellaneous orders entered	....	25,127
Total number of orders entered	....	31,558
Number of estates settled	....	22,250
Value of estates probated	....	$43,252,000 00
Largest number orders entered in any one day—April 15, 1895	....	642

The three largest estates were:

John B. Drake's	$2,100,000 00
John D. Caton's	2,000,000 00
E. K. Morrison's	1,850,000 00

REPORT OF JAMES PEASE,

Sheriff of Cook County.

A GIGANTIC OFFICE.

The incumbent of the shrievalty manages the most extensive and the most important office in the County. It embraces four large departments, each directed by a deputy sheriff. They are the Civil, County, and Criminal Courts, the County Jail and Executive Department. The work is increasing rapidly every year, that of 1895 being largely in excess of that of the preceding year.

LARGEST IN THE UNITED STATES.

Cook County requires a greater force of assistants in the Sheriff's Office than is demanded by the needs of New York or Philadelphia. The office was created in 1831, with James Kinzie as the first Sheriff, holding office for one year; receipts under him were about two hundred and fifty dollars ($250).

SUCCESSIVE INCUMBENTS.

James Forbes succeeded Sheriff Kinzie in 1832, and was succeeded in 1834 by Silas W. Sherman. Then followed in 1838 (after two terms), Isaac R. Gavin; in 1840, Ashbel Steele; in 1842, Samuel J. Lowe; in 1846 and 1848, Isaac Cook; in 1850, William L. Church; in 1852, Cyrus P. Bradley; 1854, James Andrews (died in 1855); 1855, James S. Beach; 1856, John L. Wilson; 1858, John Gray; 1860, A. C. Hesing; 1862, David Hammond; 1864, J. L. Beveridge; 1870, Ben Cleaves; 1872, J. M. Bradly; 1874, Francis Agnew; 1876, Charles Keni; 1878, John Hoffman; 1880, O. L. Mann; 1882, Seth F. Hanchett; 1886, C. R. Matson; 1890, J. R. Gilbert; 1894, James Pease.

SYNOPSIS OF BUSINESS, 1895.

The record of the Cook County Jail takes precedence and shows: Total number of prisoners booked in 1895, 5,827—452 were conveyed to Joliet, 337 to Pontiac, 2 to Chester, 1 to Northern Hospital, 352 to House of Correction, 131 had Jail sentences, 49 were incarcerated in the Debtors' Department and 17 were sent to Homes for Juvenile Offenders at Geneva. This makes a total of their delinquents of 1,321.

CASES OF INSANITY.

Thirty-two thousand and two (32,002) miles were covered in trying and conveying insane persons to different State institutions. The total number of arrests were 1,199, and the cases tried were 1,114. There were 649 pauper cases and 485 other kinds. 588 were taken to Jefferson, 164 to Elgin, 113 to Kankakee, and 77 were cared for by friends.

WRITS RECEIVED AND DISPOSED OF.

There were as follows:

Mesne process, 21,555; executions, 8,700; Criminal Courts, 41,853; Civil Courts, 38,083. Total, 110,191 writs of all kinds.

CRIMINAL COURT BUSINESS.

Capiases issued to the extent of 8,053—7,706 arrests were made, 40,121 subpœnas served, 30,386 jurors summoned, 1,475,715 miles were traveled and $163,-434.49 was earned in fees.

SHERIFF'S REPORT.

Sheriff's semi-annual financial report for the six months ending May 31, 1895:

SUMMARY.

RECEIPTS.

Final Process Account	$ 7,444 97	
Mesne Process Account	10,681 90	
Probate Court Account	759 00	
Other Court Accounts	755 65	
Sundry Fee Account	218 17	
State Auditor Mileage Account	175 00	
Total receipts		$ 29,034 69

EXPENDITURES.

REBATES.

(This item paid by Requisition No. 1,129, submitted July 16, 1895.)

Fees rebated and recording certificates	$ 1,976 83	
Sheriff, salary, six months	3,000 00	
Attorney fees, six months	1,250 00	
Balance due Cook County		$ 22,393 80
Add amount to be paid by requisition No. 1,129, submitted July 16, 1895		414 06
Due Cook County		$ 22,807 86

FINAL PROCESS ACCOUNT.

RECEIPTS.

December, 1894	$ 720 27	
January, 1895	1,561 25	
February, 1895	1,316 97	
March, 1895	1,467 84	
April, 1895	1,397 41	
May, 1895	981 23	
		$ 7,444 97

DISBURSEMENTS—REBATES.

December, 1894	$ 221 80	
January, 1895	285 50	
February, 1895	240 85	
March, 1895	226 95	
April and May, 1895	491 80	
		1,466 90
		$ 5,978 07

MESNE PROCESS ACCOUNT.

RECEIPTS.

December, 1894	$ 3,281 20	
January, 1895	3,638 10	
February, 1895	3,063 15	
March, 1895	3,199 75	
April, 1895	2,703 00	
May, 1895	3,796 70	
		$ 19,681 90

DISBURSEMENTS—REBATES.

December, 1894	$ 96 80	
January, 1895	1 77	
February, 1895	57 83	
March, 1895	58 00	
April, 1895	83 30	
May, 1895	37 00	
		509 93
		$ 19,171 97

PROBATE COURT ACCOUNT.

RECEIPTS.

December, 1894	$ 101 00	
January, 1895	102 00	
February, 1895	133 00	
March, 1895	133 00	
April, 1895	95 00	
May, 1895	195 00	
		$ 759 00

CHIEF BAILIFF ACCOUNT.

RECEIPTS.

December, 1894	$ 120 75	
January, 1895	195 45	
February, 1895	181 50	
March, 1895	122 10	
April, 1895	135 85	
		$ 755 65

EXPENSE ACCOUNT.

DISBURSEMENTS.

Sheriff's salary, December, 1894	$ 500 00	
Sheriff's salary, January, 1895	500 00	
Sheriff's salary, February, 1895	500 00	
Sheriff's salary, March, 1895	500 00	
Sheriff's salary, April, 1895	500 00	
Sheriff's salary, May, 1895	500 00	
		$ 3,000 00
Attorney's salary, January, 1895	$ 250 00	
Attorney's salary, February, 1895	250 00	
Attorney's salary, March, 1895	250 00	
Attorney's salary, April, 1895	250 00	
Attorney's salary, May, 1895	250 00	
		1,250 00
		$ 4,250 00

RECEIPTS.

Mileage, State Auditor, January, 1895	$ 175 00	
		$ 175 00
Appropriation for transportation for months of February, March, April and May exhausted.		
Paid from other fees received		$ 4,489 06

CRIMINAL COURT FEES.

The total number of writs served during said period was 29,703; total number miles traveled, 235,977, and fees earned, $29,720.25.

SIX MONTHS ENDING MAY 31, 1895.

	CAPIASES.					JURORS.				
	Writs Received.	Arrests Made.	Not Arrested.	Miles Traveled.	Fees Earned.	Writs Received.	Persons Served.	Not Found	Miles Traveled.	Fees Earned.
December	692	678	14	5,330	$1,691 20	389	342	47	3,777	$ 274 35
January	673	556	27	5,284	1,443 50	480	424	56	4,145	313 25
February	538	527	11	4,542	1,334 90	1,069	931	138	9,223	693 90
March	786	778	8	4,988	1,884 00	735	648	87	5,371	480 55
April	598	580	18	3,486	1,394 10	868	757	87	5,209	449 70
May	796	766	30	5,068	1,865 00	1,050	997	53	8,096	654 05
Total	4,083	3,885	108	28,688	$9,612 70	4,561	4,099	362	36,821	$2,865 80

	SUBPŒNAS, ETC.					TOTAL.				
	Writs Received.	Persons Served.	Not Found.	Miles Traveled.	Fees Earned.	Writs Received.	Persons Served.	Not Found	Miles Traveled.	Fees Earned.
December	1,546	3,513	209	24,871	$ 2,627 70	2,627	4,533	270	33,968	$ 4,593 25
January	1,927	3,546	220	25,235	2,695 55	3,080	4,526	303	34,664	4,432 30
February	1,636	3,379	300	25,241	2,608 30	3,243	4,837	349	39,006	4,637 10
March	1,965	3,294	160	26,488	2,673 80	3,486	4,720	255	37,847	5,038 35
April	1,889	3,160	208	28,705	2,730 15	3,325	4,497	307	37,400	2,573 95
May	2,209	4,827	196	39,928	3,906 75	4,055	6,590	279	53,092	6,425 80
Total	11,172	21,719	1,293	170,468	$17,242 25	19,816	29 703	1,763	235,977	$29,720 75

CIRCUIT, SUPERIOR AND COUNTY COURTS.

The work of this department shows a marked increase over that of similar periods of previous year.

The increase in the number of arrests made arises largely from the fact that in a majority of cases in which the defendant is admitted to bail the bonds are forfeited and the defendants arrested as many as three times before a final disposition is made of the case.

SUMMARY SIX MONTHS ENDING NOVEMBER 30, 1895.

SUMMARY.

RECEIPTS.

Final Process Account	$ 7,250 81	
Mesne Process Account	20,404 90	
Sundry Fee Account	212 80	
Probate Court Account	1,369 55	
Other Court Accounts	1,544 54	
State Auditor Mileage Account	3,145 15	
Total Receipts		$ 33,927 75

DISBURSEMENT—REBATES.

Fees Rebating and Recording Certificates	$ 2,502 99	
Sheriff's Salary, six months	3,000 00	
Attorney's Fees	1,750 00	
		7,252 99
Balance due Cook County		$ 26,674 76

REPORT OF JAMES McHALE,

Coroner of Cook County.

Coroner McHale's record of the year 1895 is of permanent interest and is concisely summed up as below:

Total number of cases investigated during the year 1895, 2381. Total number of certificates issued by Coroner's Physician, 343.

TOTAL NUMBER OF POST MORTEMS HELD BY CORONER'S PHYSICIAN.

INQUESTS BY MONTHS.—January 131, February 131, March 139, April 190, May 192, June 182, July 225, August 183, September 181, October 171, November 167, December 146.

AGE.—Under 5 years 179, 5 to 10 years 79, 10 to 20 years 159, 20 to 30 years 366, 30 to 40 years 475, 40 to 50 years 331, 50 to 60 years 238, 60 to 70 years 124, 70 to 80 years 63, over 80 years 17, not ascertained 7.

SEX AND SOCIAL CONDITION.—Male 1,652, female 386, married 827, single 750, widows 51, widowers 105, not ascertained 197, divorced 8.

RACES.—White 1,974, Colored 64.

NATIVITY.—America 882, Germany 373, Switzerland 15, not ascertained 152, Denmark 12, England 43, Canada 46, France 7, Prussia 2, Ireland 200, Russia 27, Italy 25, Austria 32, Sweden 80, Poland 22, Bohemia 55, Norway 26, Scotch 21, Holland 10, Australia 1, West Indies 2, Greece 1, Turkey 1, China 2, Finland 1.

OCCUPATIONS.—Architect 3, agent 12, actor 1, banker 1, brass finisher 2, bridge builder 3, butcher 13, broker 6, brewer 4, bricklayer 14, bartender 7, brushmaker 1, bookkeeper 11, blacksmith 15, bookbinder 4, baker 3, barber 9, brakeman 6, contractor 7, capitalist 1, conductor 6, candler 1, cabinet maker 4, carpenter 57, clerk 44, cook 12, coachman 1, city employe 1, cigarmaker 9, cooper 6, canvasser 2, cashier 1, car repairer 1, cornice maker 3, collector 3, chemist 1, confectioner 3, coppersmith 1, cash boy 1, calciminer 2, carpet cleaner 1, domestic 36, detective 1, druggist 7, dressmaker 3, elevator boy 5, expressman 6, engineer 17, engraver 1, electrician 2, errand boy 1, floor walker 1, flagman 5, farmer 17, fireman 19, foreman 4, factory girl 1, florist 1, frame maker 1, furnisher 3, fisherman 3, gardener 3, grocer 8, glazier 3, gambler 4, housewife 141, helper 2, housekeeper 28, hotel keeper 4, hatter 2, hostler 4, horseshoer 1, horseman 1, iron worker 19, inspector 7, inventor 1, iceman 2, jockey 1, jeweler 2, janitor 4, junk dealer 2, laborer 411, lamplighter 1, laundress 4, laundryman 4, lather 2, locksmith 1, motorman 1, manufacturer 8, milkman 3, manager 2, mechanic 1, machinist 21, merchant 24, musician 7, moulder 3, miner 2, mason 1, milliner 1, not ascertained 102, none 298, newsman 3, nurse 7, newsboy 2, notion dealer 1, office boy 1, oiler 1, porter 16, painter 21, police officer 8, peddler 17, plumber 10, physician 9, printer 11, packer 4, photographer 1, plasterer 2, publisher 1, polisher 1, paver 1, pilot 1, plater 1, roofer 3, reporter 2, railroad man 6, real estate dealer 1, restaurant keeper 1, shoe dealer 1, student 2, shoemaker 17, switchman 27, seamstress 3, stenographer 3, salesman 16, sailor 19, saloon keeper 18, school girl 9, superintendent 2, school boy 60, secretary 1, sign hanger 1, steward 2, sporting woman 6, stonemason 10, solicitor 3, stockman 2, soldier 1, saleslady 1, steamfitter 1, tailor 24, teamster 71, tanner 3, trunkmaker 2, trimmer 1, tinsmith 5, teacher 1, telegraph operator 1, tailoress 1, tuck pointer 1, undertaker 1, upholsterer 2, window cleaner 1, waiter 15, weigher 2, watchman 8, washwoman 1, wagon boy 2, wagon maker 1, waitress 1, wireworker 1, woodworker 4, yardmaster 3.

CAUSES OF DEATH.—Appoplexy 17, abortion 13, alcoholism 47, asphyxiation 29, asthma 6, Bright's disease 16, burns by fire 86, bronchitis 2, blood poisoning 7, bursting steam pipe 3, bursting emery wheel 2, crushed or struck by falling material 75, consumption 23, convulsions 12, cut by glass 1, cholera infantum 3, cut accidentally 2, diphtheria 3, dropsy 2, drowning (cause unknown) 76, drowning (cause accidental) 77, exposure 17, explosion 14, electrocuted 4, erysipelas 3, elevator accident 25, epelipsy 7, fracture of skull (accidental) 4, fracture of leg (accidental) 2, falls (miscellaneous) 172, fractured ribs (cause unknown) 1, falling building 4, enteritics 1, gastritis 1, homicide 126, heart disease 97, hemorrhage of lungs and brains 20, hydrophobia 1, inflammation of bowels 5, inanition 4, kicked by horse 8, lockjaw 14, machinery accident 13, meningitis 2, malarial fever 1, neuralgia 1, natural causes 3, old age 26, pneumonia 43, poison (cause unknown) 19, poisoning (cause accidental) 41, puerperal fever 1, peritonitis 3, paralysis 1, premature birth 1, R. R. accidents 275, run over by wagon or buggy 33, rupture 4, run over by bicycle 1, rheumatism 1, suicides 378, street car accidents 64, scalded 29, shooting (cause accidental) 23, shooting (cause unknown) 3, suffocated 14, struck by lightning 3, sunstroke 8, struck by blasted stone 2, stabbing (accidental) 3, syncope 1, typhoid fever 3, unknown causes 2, thrown from buggy 2, thermic fever 2.

RAILROAD ACCIDENTS—Passengers 7, employes 55, other than passengers or employes 213.

CAUSES—At crossing of street 114, falling off train 7, walking on tracks 96, jumping on or off train in motion 6, crushed by cars 11, elevated road 4, working on tracks 29, wreck (train leaving track) 6, collision 1, not ascertained 1.

SUICIDES—January 24, February 25, March 41, April 48, May 33, June 31, July 31, August 36, September 33, October 28, November 24, December 24.

AGES—10 to 20 years 17, 20 to 30 years 71, 30 to 40 years 102, 40 to 50 years 78, 50 to 60 years 69, 60 to 70 years 29, 70 to 80 years 11, over 80 years 1.

SEX, SOCIAL CONDITION AND RACES—Male 297, female 81, white 376, colored 2, married 227, single 93, widows 6, widowers 25, not ascertained 22, divorced 5.

NATIVITY—America 121, Germany 121, not ascertained 17, Norway 9, Austria 10, England 9, Ireland 20, Denmark 8, Sweden 10, Bohemia 25, Russia 5, Poland 4, Scotland 4, Holland 4, Canada 8, Switzerland 2, Italy 1.

OCCUPATIONS—Domestic 15, musician 3, laborer 50, waiter 3, mechanic 1, student 1, newsman 1, moulder 3, merchant 10, porter 1, housewife 37, butcher 3, carpenter 11, brewer 3, not ascertained 11, yard master 1, fireman 1, foreman 1, engineer 4, saloon keeper 7, iron worker 4, machinist 5, salesman 3, factory girl 1, watchman 2, none 11, junk dealer 2, clerk 14, expressman 1, housekeeper 9, peddler 6, bricklayer 3, cook 3, farmer 5, undertaker 1, blacksmith 3, druggist 2, bartender 2, printer 7, broker 4, cigar maker 3, grocer 6, bookkeeper 2, mason 1, trimmer 1, milkman 2, steward 1, tailor 12, manager 2, calciminer 1, barber 2, speculator 1, lithographer 1, polisher 1, teamster 7, horseshoer 1, waitress 2, physician 2, cabinet maker 3, nurse 3, shoemaker 3, painter 4, tanner 2, iceman 1, box dealer 1, laundress 1, cashier 1, hatter 2, finisher 1, teacher 1, agent 3, packer 1, banker 1, plumber 1, police officer 2, solicitor 2, sailor 3, laundryman 1, plasterer 1, cigar dealer 1, steamfitter 1, upholsterer 1, sporting woman 3, manufacturer 4, contractor 3, collector 1, switchman 2, railroad man 1, cooper 2, tailoress 1, brassworker 1, janitor 2, wagon maker 1, architect 1, car driver 1, notion dealer 1, woodworker 1, glazier 1, bookbinder 1, confectioner 1, canvasser 1, baker 1, inspector 1, stonemason 1, restaurant keeper 1, hostler 1.

MANNER OF DEATHS.- Asphyxiation 23, shooting 116, poisoning 146, hanging 52, cutting throat 11, stabbing 2, jumping out window 3, drowning 16, cutting artery 1, throwing under train 6, burned by acid 1, setting clothing on fire 1.

PROBABLE CAUSES.—Despondency 304, not ascertained 7, temporary insanity 65, insane 1, delirium tremens 1.

POISONS USED.—Atropia 1, narcotic 18, carbolic acid 64, strychnine 2, morphine 24, rough on rats 13, arsenic 4, laudanum 4, paris green 13, not ascertained 1, corrosive sublimate 1, opium 1.

HOMICIDES.—Shooting 80, cutting throat 2, struck on head 22, stabs or cuts 13. drowned 2, asphyxiated 5, kicked 1, thrown from train 1.

HELD TO GRAND JURY.—Murder 47, as accessory 26, criminal carelessness 23, abortion 6.

GENERAL SUMMARY.—Known parties to be apprehended 11, unknown parties to be apprehended 14, unknown parties to be apprehended for abortion 1, justifiable homicides 16, murder and suicide 2.

SEMI-ANNUAL FINANCIAL REPORTS OF CORONER McHALE FOR 1895, FIRST SIX MONTHS.

Financial report of the transactions of the Coroner's office for the term commencing December 1, 1894, and ending May 31, 1895, in accordance with Chapter 53, Section 31 of the Revised Statutes of the State of Illinois:

Post mortem held by doctors	226
Total inquests and investigations	1,112

RECAPITULATION.

RECEIPTS.

Fees collected on writs	$ 299 30	
Fees collected on inquests	605 71	
Fees collected on certified copies, etc	70 85	
Total		$ 975 86

EXPENSES.

Transportation, attorney fees, telegrams, etc	$ 500 00	
		500 00
		$475 86

SECOND SIX MONTHS.

INQUESTS.

June	182	
July	225	
August	185	
September	181	
October	171	
November	167	
		1,111

INVESTIGATIONS.

June	21	
July	24	
August	23	
September	22	
October	27	
November	29	
		146

Post-mortems held by doctor, 289.

Total inquests and investigations	1,257

WRITS SERVED DURING SIX MONTHS.

June	22	
July	30	
August	24	
September	33	
October	50	
November	36	
		195

FEES COLLECTED.

On writs—		
June	$ 42 25	
July	47 25	
August	33 25	
September	36 75	
October	75 00	
November	53 25	
		$ 287 75
On inquests—		
June	$ 114 00	
July	96 00	
August	90 00	
September	30 00	
October	66 00	
November	60 00	
		456 00
Certified copies, etc		84 05
Total		$ 827 80

RECAPITULATION.

RECEIPTS.

Fees collected on writs	$ 287 75	
Fees collected on iuquests	456 00	
Certified copies, etc	84 05	
		827 80

EXPENDITURES.

Transportation, attoruey fees, telegrams, etc., as per attached statement	$ 500 00	
		500 00
Amount due Cook County		$ 327 80

REPORT OF COUNTY TREASURER.

The duties of the County Treasurer are to act as Custodian of the County funds, to pay out moneys on the order of the County Board, to receive money paid in on orders from the various Courts, and pay them out on proper instructions; but this is only a very small part of his duties. As Ex-Officio County Collector he is the official upon whom devolves the task of collecting all taxes and special assessments levied in the County, and it is this position which makes his office so responsible and onerous.

STATE AND COUNTY TAXES.

There are thirty-three towns in this County, each with a full set of town officers, viz.: Assessor, Collector, supervisor, and Town Clerk. The Assessor of each town gets from the County Clerk in March of each year a list of all the taxable real estate in his town and after placing a valuation upon each lot or tract of land returns his books to the County Clerk. After the returns are all in the County Board examines them and equalizes the valuation of both real and personal property, having the authority to add to or deduct from the valuation of both or either class of property in any town, but without changing the aggregate valuation in the County. After the books are examined and proved by the County Clerk, a statement of the valuation of the county is sent to the State Auditor at Springfield and by him laid before State Board of Equalization, which meets in August each year and whose duty it is to equalize the valuation as between Counties on real and personal property, and to fix the valuation of all railroad property in the State. These gentlemen invariably add largely to the valuation of Cook County, the rates of addition made being in 1894 as follows: Lots 18 per cent, lands 39 per cent, personal property 43 per cent. In 1895: Lots 17 per cent, lands 20 per cent, personal property 19 per cent. When the work of the State Board is finished its result is certified to the County Clerk, and on the valuation thus established the rates are made and the taxes extended in the various towns. When the warrants for a town are finished they are turned over to the Collector after his bond (which must be double the amount of the total taxes extended) has been filed and he holds possession of the books and collects taxes until the 10th of March, when his commission expires, and he then prepares his delinquent lists and turns his book over to the County Collector. As they collect up to March 10 and as in some of the towns there is a great deal of labor involved in making the delinquent list, the warrants are not all in the hands of the County Collector, examined, proved and ready to be placed in collection before the 1st of April. On that date special assessments must be returned, and to mark these up on the warrants and check them back, so as to be able to give bills for everything there may be against a given piece of property, requires about ten days working night and day, and as a penalty of 1 per cent is added on May 1, which everybody is anxious to escape, every night and every Sunday during the month of April and the first half of May finds every clerk in the Collector's office (and many outsiders pressed into service) at work. Every bill left in the office with check before May 1 escapes the penalty, and it takes working as above stated, days, nights and Sundays, until the middle of May to work off these accumulations and attend to the daily business over the counter.

Under the law the Collector applies to the County Court each year at the July term for judgment and order for sale on all unpaid real estate taxes and special assessments, and just as soon as the above work is done a large force is put on at night from 5:00 to 11:30 copying for the printers and making the judgment record. Some idea may be formed of the amount of this labor when we say that the delinquent list last year filled 141 pages of the *Chicago Mail*, seven columns to the page, and that the tax judgment and redemption record embraced 185 volumes, averaging 150 pages each.

On the second Monday in July each year the Collector applies to the County Court for judgment, and early in August the tax sale commences on all property on which judgment has been rendered, which sale generally runs into December each year before it is finished. The accompanying table will show the number of certificates issued and amount of sales in 1895 for general taxes and for each taxing corporation that returned delinquent special assessments that year.

TAX SALE.

CORPORATION.	Certificates.	Amount.
State and County	45,248	$517,693 10
West Park Specials	193	21,099 03
Lincoln Park Specials	19	23,219 97
Village of Bartlett Specials	8	106 08
Village of Blue Island Specials	137	2,471 00
Town of Cicero specials	5,487	36,512 35
Village of Chicago Heights Specials	103	1,226 40
Village of Desplaines Specials	20	319 46
City of Evanston Specials	640	14,960 30
Village of Glencoe Specials	169	1,042 69
Village of Harlem Specials	251	1,379 06
Village of Harvey Specials	757	4,244 85
Village of Lansing Specials	7	754 40
Village of La Grange Specials	721	6,985 99
Village of La Grange Park Specials	27	496 82
Village of Maywood Specials	130	890 67
Village of Melrose Park Specials	782	4,058 30
Village of Morgan Park Specials	1,833	7,137 36
Village of North Harvey Specials	85	695 92
Town of Orland (Drainage)	4	388 12
Village of Park Ridge Specials	434	3,788 82
Village of River Forest Specials	142	1,981 82
Village of River Grove Specials	3	61 96
Village of Riverside Specials	270	6,562 34
Village of Western Springs Specials	333	2,057 97
Village of Winnetka Specials	230	2,717 15
Village of Willmette Specials	1,130	11,319 85
City of Chicago Specials	13,367	284,951 13
Totals	72,530	$959,122 90

SPECIAL ASSESSMENTS.

For collecting regular taxes the County Collector gets 1 per cent and the same for special assessments, which involves five times as much labor, and in the case of assessments levied on the installment plan much more than that. Under the law the collection of special assessments cannot be enforced unless they are in the hands of the County Collector by April 1, and the majority of all cities, towns and villages making assessments wait until the last day, forcing the work of marking them up on the regular tax warrants on the office at a time when it is already crowded with work. There are outside of the three Park Records in the County over thirty corporations authorized to levy assessments, and nearly all of them take advantage of their rights, and the number of assessments returned, especially by the country villages, is increasing from year to year.

The following table will show the amount of general taxes returned for collections in 1895, and the number of volumes and also the number of warrants and amount of special assessments returned:

TAXES AND ASSESSMENTS RETURNED.

	No. Volumes.	No. Warrants.	No. Institutions.	Total Amount Returned for Collection.
General Taxes 1894	331	....	....	$12,228,457 17
Railroad Warrant	3	....	....	2,206,670 97
Special Assessments.				
West Park	7	7	7	210,767 35
Lincoln Park	2	2	2	72,203 25
City of Chicago	106	2	246	3,889,586 09
Bartlett	1	1,433	....	101 80
Blue Island	2	1	7	13,817 80
Cicero	13	16	116	268,753 32
Chicago Heights	3	162	4	19,020 55
Desplaines	1	9	....	1,531 36
Evanston	5	82	59	168,871 79
Glencoe	1	3	3	18,279 38
Harlem	2	12	6	15,219 54
Harvey	4	31	15	25,262 69
Lansing	1	2	....	1,764 39
LaGrange	4	72	57	66,827 16
LaGrange Park	2	2	1	3,176 74
Maywood	2	14	11	9,486 27
Melrose	3	27	20	14,621 64
Morgan Park	9	41	37	55,687 53
North Harvey	1	7	7	4 853 15
Park Ridge	3	29	19	18,640 57
Riverside	1	17	9	33,203 65
River Forest	2	25	14	40,130 13
Western Springs	1	12	12	31,808 94
Wilmette	7	16	6	133,994 99
Winnetka	2	16	4	39,261 25
Drainage—Orland	1	2	2	808 98
Drainage—Orland and Bremen	1	1	1	29 83
Drainage—Bremen	1	1	1	251 53
Drainage—Niles	1	1	1	336 40
River Grove	1	1	1	314 89
Total	524	2,171	668	$18,593,742 10

RAILROAD TAXES.

The valuation of each road in the County is made by the State Board of Equalization for the following classes of property:

(1) Main track right of way and improvements on right of way; (2) second track; (3) side track; (4) rolling stock; (5) personal property other than rolling stock; and by them certified to the County Clerk, and the taxes extended by towns and villages in the same way and on the same rates as real and personal property. Real estate outside of the right of way is assessed by the local Assessor at the same rate of valuation as other real property. The railroad tax warrants, when finished by the County Clerk, are given directly to the County Collector instead of passing through the hands of the Town Collectors. The following table will show the amount of railroad taxes extended for 1895:

RAILROAD TAXES.

Pennsylvania Line (P. F. W. & C.)	$145,257 87
Chicago & Northern Pacific	134,740 96
Pittsburg, Cincinnati, Chicago & St. Louis	121,860 31
Chicago & Northwestern	120,524 04
Chicago & Western Indiana	118,536 50
Chicago, Rock Island & Pacific	95,819 71
Union Stock Yards Railroad and Transit Company	93,218 60
Lake Shore & Michigan Southern	86,555 98
Chicago, Burlington & Quincy	77,058 73
Chicago, Milwaukee & St. Paul	74,877 30
Chicago & Grand Trunk	57,573 35
Chicago & Western Indiana (Belt Line)	55,470 55

New York, Chicago & St. Louis	$ 36,862 81
Chicago, Alton & St. Louis	31,869 06
Chicago, Santa Fe & California	31,056 20
Chicago & South Side Rapid Transit Company	29,788 67
Grand Trunk Junction	29,643 87
Calumet & Blue Island	29,583 62
Metropolitan West Side Elevated	23,065 86
Baltimore & Ohio & Chicago	17,471 60
Lake Street Elevated	15,980 23
Wabash	13,583 21
Michigan Central	13,245 39
Chicago & Eastern Illinois	13,214 91
Chicago, Madison & Northern	13,134 59
Chicago & Calumet Terminal	11,607 70
Wisconsin Central	9,817 42
Elgin, Joliet & Eastern	7,289 84
South Chicago	7,243 18
Chicago Union Transfer Company	6,789 97
Michigan Central (J. & N. I. Line)	4,524 44
Chicago & Erie	4,111 15
Baltimore & Ohio Connecting	3,805 08
Chicago & Indiana State Line	3,734 34
Chicago Great Western	3,719 15
Chicago & Northwestern Junction	3,664 84
South Chicago & Southern	3,532 98
Englewood Connecting	2,479 22
Louisville, New Albany & Chicago	2,381 26
Calumet River	2,080 59
Blue Island	1,619 20
Chicago & Illinois Southern	181 33
Total	$1,558,575 61

QUARTERLY AND SEMI-ANNUAL REPORTS OF THE COUNTY TREASURER.

OUTSTANDING ORDER FUND.

DR.

To balance Dec. 3, 1894		$ 3,783 92

CR.

By amount transferred to Funding Fund account	$ 1,874 23	
By paid orders	50 00	
By commissions on disbursements, ½ per cent on $50 00	25	
		$ 1,924 48
By Balance		1,859 44
		$ 3,783 92
To balance March 1, 1895		$ 1,859 44
Orders outstanding		1,830 15

FUNDING FUND ACCOUNT.

DR.

To balance Dec. 3, 1894		$ 23,686 16
The amount from outstanding Order Fund		1,874 23
To amount received of Jas. L. Monaghan, Deputy Comptroller	$ 847 70	
To amount dep. account Clerk Circuit Court (unclaimed fees)	1,180 16	
To amount dep. account Clerk Superior Court (unclaimed fees)	336 75	
		2,364 61
		$ 27,925 00

CR.

By paid orders	$ 822 75	
By commissions on receipts, ½ per cent on $2,364.61	11 82	
By commission on disbursements, ½ per cent on $922.75	4 61	
		$ 939 18
Balance		26,985 82
		$ 27,925 00
To balance March 1, 1895		$ 26,985 82

INTEREST FUND—OLD INDEBTEDNESS.

DR.

To balance Dec. 3, 1894		$ 78,042 85

CR.

By paid Refunding bond coupons	$ 4,629 25	
By commissions on disbursements, ½ per cent on $4,629 25	23 14	
		$ 4,652 39
By balance		73,390 46
		$ 78,042 85
To balance March 1, 1895		$ 73,290 46

INTEREST FUND—NEW INDEBTEDNESS.

DR.

To balance Dec. 3, 1894		$ 19,432 11

CR.

By paid Court House bond coupons ....$	13,975 00	
By paid Funding Bond coupons	1,680 00	
By paid Refunding bond coupons	1,100 00	
	$	16,755 00
By commissions on disbursements, ½ per cent on $16,755.00..........		83 77
By balance.............		2,593 34
	$	19,432 11
To balance March 1, 1895.	$	2,593 34

FUNDING BOND ACCOUNT.

DR.

To balance Dec. 3, 1894...	$	1,100 00

CR.

By paid bonds............	$	1,000 00
By balance..............		100 00
	$	1,100 00
To balance March 1, 1895.	$	100 00
Bond outstanding........		100 00

TAVERN LICENSE.

DR.

To balance Dec. 3, 1894..	$	4,295 18
To received for license..		1,491 67
	$	5,786 85

CR.

By paid orders..........	$	2,126 25
By balance		3,660 60
	$	5,786 85
To balance March 1, 1895.	$	3,660 60

EMERGENCY FUND.

DR.

To balance Dec. 3, 1894..	$	333 40

CR.

By amount transferred to General Fund account.	$	333 40

GENERAL FUND ACCOUNT.

DR.

To balance Dec. 3, 1894.	$	33,396 04
To amount received County tax		143,798 90
To amount from Emergency Fund...........		333 40
To amount from County Treasurer, Commissioner's account...........		8,969 06
To amount from County Collectors, cost account		34,373 20
To amount from J. H. Gilbert, late Sheriff......$	6,609 43	
To amount from F. J. Gaulter, Clerk Circuit Court	49,600 17	
To amount from H. Wulff late County Clerk.....	73,188 10	
To amount from James McHale, Coroner......$	417 87	
To amount from S. D. Griffin, Clerk Superior Ct..	24,493 38	
So amount from R. C. Sullivan, late Clerk Probate Court	3,268 11	
To amount from J. C. Shubert, late Clerk Criminal Court............	322 35	
	$	157,899 41
	$	378,770 01

CR.

By amount Credited Salary Fund, 1894........$	93,633 66	
By amount credited Supply Fund, 1894........	61,881 55	
By amount credited Building Fund, 1894........	32,133 30	
By amount credited Miscellaneous Fund, 1894.	25,741 48	
By amount credited Contingent Fund, 1894....	1,088 82	
By amount credited Salary Fund, 1895........	104,124 52	
By amount credited Supply Fund, 1895........	39,705 41	
By amount credited Building Fund, 1895........	38 73	
By amount credited Miscellaneous Fund, 1895.	2,346 00	
By amount credited Contingent Fund, 1895....	4,461 53	
	$	365,155 00
By commissions on receipts, ½ per cent on $157,899.41		789 50
By balance.............		12,825 51
	$	378,770 01
To balance March 1, 1895	$	12,825 51

SALARY FUND, 1894.

DR.

To balance Dec. 3, 1894..	$	68,567 43
To amount from General Fund account.........		93,633 66
	$	192,201 09

CR.

By paid orders..........$	159,599 95	
By commissions on disbursements, ½ per cent on $159,599.95	798 00	
	$	160,397 95
By balance		1,803 14
	$	162,201 09
To balance March 1, 1895	$	1,803 14
Orders outstanding		1,794 18

SUPPLY FUND, 1894.

DR.

To balance Dec. 3, 1894..	$	23,533 79
To amount from General Fund account.........		61,881 55
	$	85,415 34

CR.

By paid orders..........	$ 84,206 70	
By commissions on disbursements, ½ per cent on $84,206.70..........	421 03	
		$ 84,627 73
By balance.............		787 61
		$ 85,415 34
To balance March 1, 1895		$ 787 61
Orders outstanding......		783 70

BUILDING FUND, 1894.

DR.

To balance Dec. 3, 1894..		$ 17,467 20
To amount from General Fund account........		32,133 30
		$ 49,600 50

CR.

By amount transferred to Building Fund, 1895...		$ 6,569 93
By paid orders		42,807 16
By commissions on disbursements, ½ per cent on $42,807.16		214 04
By balance.............		9 37
		$ 49,600 50
To balance March 1, 1895		$ 9 37
Orders outstanding		9 33

MISCELLANEOUS FUND, 1894.

DR.

To balance Dec. 3, 1894..		$ 2,377 94
To amount from General Fund account.........		25,741 48
		$ 28,119 42

CR.

By paid orders..........	$ 26,922 41	
By commissions on disbursements, ½ per cent on $26,922.41	134 61	
		$ 27,057 02
By balance.............		1,062 40
		$ 28,119 42
To balance March 1, 1895		$ 1,062 40
Orders outstanding		1,057 12

CONTINGENT FUND, 1894.

DR.

To balance Dec. 3, 1894..		$ 33 15
To amount from General Fund account.........		1,088 82
		$ 1,121 97

CR.

By paid orders..........	$ 1,091 23	
By commissions on disbursements, ½ per cent on $1,091.23	5 46	
		$ 1,096 69
By balance.............		25 28
		$ 1,121 97
To balance March 1, 1895		$ 25 28
Orders outstanding......		25 28

SALARY FUND, 1895.

DR.

To amount from General Fund account.........		$ 104,124 52

CR.

By paid orders..........	$ 101,539 36	
By commissions on disbursements, ½ per cent on $101,539.36	707 70	
		$ 102,047 06
By balance..........		2,077 46
		$ 104,124 52
To balance March 1, 1895		$ 2,077 46
Orders outstanding......		2,077 46

SUPPLY FUND.

DR.

To amount from General Fund		$ 39,705 41
To amount from County Tax, 1894		904 93
Total...............		$ 40,610 34

CR.

By paid orders..........	$ 26,874 57	
By commissions on disbursements, ½ per cent on $26,874.57	134 37	
		$ 27,008 94
By balance.............		13,601 40
		$ 40,610 34
To balance March 1, 1895.		$ 13,601 40
Orders outstanding		13,601 40

BUILDING FUND, 1895.

DR.

To amount from Building Fund, 1894..........		$ 6,569 93
To amount from General fund account		38 73
To amount from County Tax, 1894............		1,367 11
		$ 7,975 77

CR.

By paid orders..........	$ 7,745 64	
By commissions on disbursements, ½ per cent on $7,745.64	38 73	
		$ 7,784 37
By balance.............		191 40
		$ 7,975 77
To balance March 1, 1895.		$ 191 40
Orders outstanding		191 40

MISCELLANEOUS FUND, 1895.

DR.

To amount from General Fund account.........		$ 2,346 00
To amount from County Tax, 1894............		483 70
		$ 2,829 70

CR.

By paid orders..........$	2,250 75	
By commissions on disbursements, ½ per cent on $2,250.75..........	11 25	
	$	2,262 00
By balance............		567 70
	$	2,829 70
To balance March 1, 1895.	$	567 70
Orders outstanding.....		567 70

CONTINGENT FUND, 1895.

DR.

To amount from General Fund account........	$	4,461 53

CR.

By paid orders..........	$	4,439 33
By commissions on disbursements, ½ per cent on $4,439.33..........		22 20
	$	4,461 53

QUARTERLY REPORT, JUNE, 1895.

OUTSTANDING ORDER FUND.

DR.

To balance March 1, 1895	$	1,859 44
To balance from Salary Fund, 1894...........$	1,803 14	
To balance from Supply Fund, 1894...........	787 61	
To balance from Building Fund, 1894...........	9 37	
To balance from Miscellaneous Fund, 1894...	1,062 40	
To balance from Contingent Fund, 1894......	25 28	
		3,687 80
	$	5,547 24

CR.

By paid orders..........$	3,067 83	
By commissions on disbursements, ½ per cent on $3,067.83......	15 34	
	$	3,083 17
By balance............		2,464 07
	$	5,547 24
To Balance June 1, 1895.	$	2,464 07
Orders outstanding.....		2,431 80

FUNDING FUND.

DR.

To Balance March 1, 1895	$	26,985 82
To amount received of J. L. Monaghan, Deputy Comptroller..........$	249 40	
To amount received for office rent...........	75 00	
		324 40
	$	27,310 22

CR.

By paid orders..........$	2,029 38	
By commissions on receipts, ½ per cent on $324.40...............	1 62	
By commissions on disbursements, ½ per cent on $2,029.38.....	10 14	
	$	2,041 14
By balance............		25,269 08
	$	27,310 22
To balance June 1, 1895.	$	25,269 08

INTEREST FUND—OLD INDEBTEDNESS.

DR.

To Balance March 1, 1895	$	73,390 46
To amount received, tax 1894.................		75,000 00
	$	148,390 46

CR.

By paid refunding bond coupons..............$	30,433 25	
By commissions on disbursements, ½ per cent on $30,433.25.....	152 16	
	$	30,585 41
By balance............		117,805 05
	$	148,390 46
To balance June 1, 1895.	$	117,805 05

INTEREST FUND—NEW INDEBTEDNESS.

DR.

To balance March 1, 1895	$	2,593 34
To amount received tax 1894.................		114,100 00
	$	116,693 34

CR.

By paid Court House bond coupons........$	690 00	
By paid funding bond coupons.............	12,156 00	
By paid refunding bond coupons.............	22,060 00	
	$	34,906 00
By commissions on disbursements, ½ per cent on $34,906.00.....		174 53
By balance............		81,612 81
	$	116,693 34
To balance June 1, 1895..	$	81,612 81

FUNDING BOND ACCOUNT.

DR.

To balance March 1, 1895.	$	100 00
To amount received tax 1894.................		50,000 00
	$	50,100 00

CR.

By paid bonds..........		$ 39,900 00
By balance....		10,200 00
		$ 50,100 00
To balance June 1, 1895.		$ 10,200 00
Bonds outstanding......		10,200 00

REFUNDING BOND ACCOUNT.

DR.

To amount received tax 1894.................		$ 67,500 00

CR.

By paid bonds..........		$ 54,500 00
By balance..............		13,000 00
		$ 67,500 00
To balance June 1, 1895.		$ 13,000 00
Bonds outstanding......		13,000 00

TAVERN LICENSE.

DR.

To balance March 1, 1895		$ 3,660 60
To amount received for licenses		1,721 47
		$ 5,382 07

CR.

By paid orders..........		$ 1,428 75
By balance..............		3,953 32
		$ 5,382 07
To balance June 1, 1895..		$ 3,953 32
Orders outstanding......		319 32

GENERAL FUND ACCOUNT.

DR.

To balance March 1, 1895	$ 12,825 51	
To amount received tax 1894.................	1,189,233 56	
To amount received interest on delinquent taxes................	7,865 61	
		$1,209,924 68

CR.

By amount credited Salary Fund, 1895........	$ 374,177 50	
By amount credited Supply Fund, 1895........	284,116 67	
By amount credited Build-Fund, 1895	9,154 71	
By amount credited Miscellaneous Fund, 1895.	59,966 55	
By amount credited Contingent Fund, 1895....	7,884 36	
		$ 735,299 79
By balance		474,624 89
		$1,209,924 68
To balance June 1, 1895.		$ 474,624 89

SALARY FUND, 1895.

DR.

To balance March 1, 1895		2,077 46
To amount from General Fund account.........		374,177 50
		$ 376,254 96

CR.

By paid orders..........$	344,387 54	
By commissions on disbursements, ½ per cent on $344,387.54	1,721 94	
		$ 346,109 48
By balance............		30,145 48
		$ 376,254 96
To balance June 1, 1895 .		$ 30,145 48
Orders outstanding.....		30,145 48

SUPPLY FUND, 1895.

DR.

To balance March 1, 1895		$ 13,601 40
To amount from General Fund account.........		284,116 67
		$ 297,718 07

CR.

By paid orders.........$	261,499 58	
By commissions on disbursements, ½ per cent on $261,499.58........	1,307 49	
		$ 262,807 07
By balance............		34,911 00
		$ 297,718 07
To balance June 1, 1895..		$ 34,911 00
Orders outstanding		34,911 00

BUILDING FUND, 1895.

DR.

To balance March 1, 1895		$ 191 40
To amount received, tax 1894.................$	21,907 21	
To amount from General Fund account.........	9,154 71	
		31,061 92
		$ 31,253 32

CR.

By paid orders..........$	30,943 21	
By commissions on disbursements, ½ per cent on $30,943.21	154 71	
		$ 31,087 92
By balance		155 40
		$ 31,253 32
To balance June 1, 1895..		$ 155 40
Orders outstanding......		155 40

MISCELLANEOUS FUND, 1895.

DR.

To balance March 1, 1895		$ 567 70
To amount from General Fund account.........$	59,966 55	
To amount received, tax 1894.................	1,350 00	
		61,316 55
		$ 61,884 25

CR.

By paid orders.........$	59,743 98	
By commissions on disbursements, ½ per cent on $59,743.98.........	298 72	
		$ 60,042 70

By balance..............		$ 1,841 55
		$ 61,884 25
To balance June 1, 1895 .		$ 1,841 55
Orders outstanding......		1,841 55

CONTINGENT FUND, 1895.

DR.

To amount from General Fund account.........		$ 7,884 36

CR.

By paid orders.........$	7,182 59	
By commissions on disbursements, ½ per cent on $7,182.59...........	35 91	$ 7,218 50
By balance..............		665 86
		$ 7,884 36
To balance June 1, 1895.		$ 665 86
Orders outstanding......		665 86

TUITION FUND.

DR.

To amount received of O. T. Bright, Co. Supt. of Schools	$ 2,538 00

CR.

By paid orders..........	$ 1,420 00
By balance..............	1,118 00
	$ 2,538 00
To balance	$ 1,118 00
Orders outstanding.....	1,010 00

LIBRARY AND APPARATUS FUND.

DR.

To amount received of O. T. Bright, Co. Supt. of Schools	$ 1,000 00

CR.

By balance	$ 1,000 00
To balance June 1, 1895.	$ 1,000 00
Orders outstanding	420 00

SEMI-ANNUAL REPORT.

of D. H. Kochersperger, County Treasurer, of the fees received by him as such Treasurer, and disbursements from same, from December 3, 1894, to June 1, 1895.

TREASURY DEPARTMENT.

COMMISSION ACCOUNT.

DR.

To balance December 3, 1895..................		$ 8,969 06
To commissions received since (see Exhibit "A")		7,073 04
		$ 16,042 10

CR.

By amount credited General Fund account.....$	8,969 06	
By paid Treasurer's salary..................	1,977 76	$ 10,946 82
By balance.............		5,095 28
		$ 16,042 10
To balance June 1, 1895 .		$ 5,095 28

COLLECTING DEPARTMENT.

COMMISSION ACCOUNT.

CR.

By paid clerk hire (see Exhibit "B").........	$ 90,403 83
Leaving amount overdrawn (for which there will be commissions to cover same)...........	90,403 83

COST ACCOUNT.

DR.

To balance December 3, 1894...	$ 34,373 20
To amount received since (see Exhibit "C").....	4,874 65
	$ 39,247 85

CR.

By amount credited General Fund account.....	$ 34,373 20
By balance..............	4,874 65
	$ 39,247 85
To balance June 1, 1895 .	$ 4,874 65

SEPTEMBER, 1895, QUARTERLY REPORT.

OUTSTANDING ORDER FUND.

DR.

To balance June 1, 1895.		$ 2,464 07

CR.

By paid orders..........$	424 94	
By commissions on disbursements, ½ per cent on $424.94...........	2 13	$ 427 07
By balance		2,037 00
		$ 2,464 07
To balance Sept. 2, 1895.		$ 2,037 00
Orders outstanding		2,006 86

FUNDING FUND.

DR.

To balance June 1, 1895..		$ 25,269 08
To amount received of J. L. Monaghan, Deputy Comptroller		353 80
		$ 25,622 88

CR.

By paid orders..........$	300 74	
By commissions on disbursements, ½ per cent on $300.74..........	1 50	
By commissions on receipts, ½ per cent on $353.80	1 77	
		$ 304 01
By balance		25,318 87
		$ 25,622 88
To balance Sept. 2, 1895.		$ 25,318 87

INTEREST FUND—OLD INDEBTEDNESS.

DR.

To balance June 1, 1895..		$ 117,805 05

CR.

By paid refunding fund bond coupons.........$	4,782 37	
By commissions on disbursements, ½ per cent on $4,782 37	23 91	
		$ 4,806 28
By balance		112,998 77
		$ 117,805 05
To balance Sept. 2, 1895.		$ 112,998 77

INTEREST FUND—NEW INDEBTEDNESS.

DR.

To balance June 1, 1895..		$ 81,612 81

CR.

By paid Court House bond coupons.........$	20,140 00	
By paid refunding bond coupons.............	710 00	
By paid funding bond coupons.............	490 00	
		$ 21,340 00
By commissions on disbursements, ½ per cent on $21,340.00..........		106 70
By balance		60,166 11
		$ 81,612 81
To balance Sept. 2, 1895.		$ 60,166 11

FUNDING BOND ACCOUNT.

DR.

To balance June 1, 1895..	$ 10,200 00

CR.

By paid bonds	$ 700 00
By balance	9,500 00
	$ 10,200 00
To balance Sept. 2, 1895.	$ 9,500 00
Bonds outstanding	9,500 00

REFUNDING BOND ACCOUNT.

DR.

To balance June 1, 1895..	$ 13,000 00

CR.

By paid bonds	$ 2,000 00
By balance	11,000 00
	$ 13,000 00
To balance Sept. 2, 1895.	$ 11,000 00
Bonds outstanding......	11,000 00

TAVERN LICENSE.

DR.

To balance June 1, 1895..	$ 3,953 32
To amount received for licenses	8,108 37
	$ 12,061 69

CR.

By paid orders.........	$ 953 07
By balance	11,108 62
	$ 12,061 69
To balance Sept. 2, 1895.	$ 11,108 62
Orders outstanding	25 00

GENERAL FUND ACCOUNT.

DR.

To balance June 1, 1895..		$474,624 89
To amount received of A. Cooper, Clerk Probate Court ....$	21,242 41	
To amount received of F. J. Gaulter, Clerk of Circuit Court	46,808 67	
To amount received of E. J. Magerstadt, Clerk of Criminal Court........	307 65	
		68,358 73
To amount received of tax, 1894		218,205 59
To amount received of interest on delinquent taxes		56,784 40
		$ 817,973 61

CR.

By amount credited Salary Fund, 1895........$	263,426 90	
By amount credited Supply Fund, 1895........	74,263 80	
By amount credited Building Fund, 1895...	20,494 05	
By amount credited miscellaneous Fund, 1895.	33,522 54	
By amount credited Contingent Fund, 1895....	1,789 82	
		$ 393,497 11
By commissions on receipts, ½ per cent on $68,358.73		341 79
By balance		424,134 71
		$ 817,973 61
To balance, Sept. 2, 1885.		$ 424,134 71

SALARY FUND, 1895.

DR.

To balance June 1, 1895..		$ 30,145 48
To amount from General Fund account.........		263,426 90
		$ 293,572 38

CR.

By paid orders..........	$ 220,787 38	
By commissions on disbursements, ½ per cent on $220,787.38	1,103 94	$ 221,891 32
By balance		71,681 06
		$ 293,572 38

SUPPLY FUND, 1895.

DR.

To balance June 1, 1895..		$ 34,911 00
To amount from General Fund account.........		74,263 80
		$ 109,174 80

CR.

By paid orders..........	$ 107,200 79	
By commissions on disbursements, ½ per cent on $107,200.79	536 00	$ 107,736 79
By balance		1,438 01
		$ 109,174 80

To balance Sept. 2, 1895.		$ 1,438 01
Orders outstanding......		1,438 01

BUILDING FUND, 1895.

DR.

To balance June 1, 1895..		$ 155 40
To amount received of tax, 1894.............		1,794 41
To amount from General Fund account.........		20,494 05
		$ 22,443 86

CR.

By paid orders..........		$ 22,332 20
By commissions on disbursements, ½ per cent on $22,332.20.........		111 66
		$ 22,243 86

MISCELLANEOUS FUND, 1895.

DR.

To balance June 1, 1895 .		$ 1,841 55
To amount from General Fund account		22,522 54
		$ 35,364 09

CR.

By paid orders..........	$ 25,298 87	
By commissions on disbursements, ½ per cent on $25,298.87	126 50	$ 25,425 37
By balance		9,938 72
		$ 35,364 09

To balance Sept. 2, 1895.		$ 9,938 72
Orders outstanding		9,938 72

CONTINGENT FUND, 1895.

DR.

To balance, June 1, 1895.		$ 665 86
To amount from General Fund account		1,789 82
		$ 2,455 68

CR.

By paid orders..........	$ 1,987 18	
By commissions on disbursements, ½ per cent on $1,987.18..........	9 94	
		$ 1,997 12
By balance		458 56
		$ 2,455 68

To balance Sept. 2, 1895.		$ 458 56
Orders outstanding......		458 56

TUITION FUND.

DR.

To balance June 1, 1895 .		$ 1,118 00
To amount received of O. T. Bright, Co. Supt. of Schools............		704 00
		$ 1,822 00

CR.

By paid orders		$ 1,820 00
By balance		2 00
		$ 1,822 00

To balance Sept. 2, 1895.		$ 2 00

LIBRARY AND APARATUS FUND.

DR.

To balance June 1, 1895.		$ 1,000 00

CR.

By paid orders		$ 906 86
By balance		93 14
		$ 1,000 00

To balance Sept. 2, 1895.		$ 93 14

DECEMBER, 1895, QUARTERLY REPORT.

OUTSTANDING ORDER FUND.

DR.

To balance Sept 2, 1895 .		$ 2,037 00

CR.

By paid orders..........	$ 242 67	
By commissions on disbursements, ½ per cent on $242.67	1 21	$ 243 88
By balance		1,793 12
		$ 2,037 00

To balance Dec. 1, 1895..		$ 1,793 12
Orders outstanding		1,764 14

FUNDING FUND.

DR.

To balance Sept. 2, 1895		$ 25,318 87
To amount received of J. L. Monaghan, Deputy Comptroller		345 00
		$ 25,663 87

CR.

By paid orders ....$	38 35	
By commissions on disbursements, ½ per cent on $38.35............	19	
By commission on receipts, ½ per cent on $45.00	1 72	
		$ 40 26
By balance.............		25,623 61
		$ 25,663 87

To balance Dec. 1, 1895..		$ 25,623 61
Orders outstanding.....		110 00

INTEREST FUND—OLD INDEBTEDNESS.

DR.

To Balance Sept. 2, 1895.		$ 112,998 77

CR.

By paid refunding bond coupons ....$	30,376 25	
By commissions on disbursements, ½ per cent on $30,376.25	151 88	
		$ 30,528 13
By balance.............		82,470 64
		$ 112,998 77

To balance Dec. 1, 1895..		$ 82,470 64

INTEREST FUND—NEW INDEBTEDNESS.

DR.

To balance Sept. 2, 1895.		$ 60,166 11

CR.

By paid Court House bond coupons.........$	1,925 00	
By paid Refunding bond coupons..............	23,000 00	
By paid Funding bond coupons..............	13,334 00	
		$ 38,259 00
By commissions on disbursements, ½ per cent on $38,259.00.........		191 29
By balance..............		21,715 82
		$ 60,166 11

To balance Dec. 1, 1895.		$ 21,715 82

FUNDING BOND ACCOUNT.

DR.

To balance Sept. 2, 1895.		$ 9,500 00

CR.

By paid bonds..........$	9,400 00	
By balance..............	100 00	
		$ 9,500 00

To balance Dec. 1, 1895..		$ 100 00
Bond outstanding.......		100 00

REFUNDING BOND ACCOUNT.

DR.

To balance Sept. 2, 1895.		$ 11 000 00

CR.

By paid bonds..........$	9,000 00	
By balance.............	2,000 00	
		$ 11,000 00

To balance Dec. 1, 1895..		$ 2,000 00
Bonds outstanding.......		2,000 00

TAVERN LICENSE.

DR.

To balance Sept. 2, 1895.		$ 11,108 62
To amount received for license		3,183 37
		$ 14,291 99

CR.

By paid orders..........$	8,895 00	
By amount transferred to General Fund account	3,961 99	
		$ 12,856 99
By balance.............		1,435 00
		$ 14,291 99

To balance Dec, 1, 1895.		$ 1,435 00
Orders outstanding......		160 00

GENERAL FUND ACCOUNT.

DR.

To balance Sept. 2, 1895.		$ 424,134 71
To amount received of S. D. Griffin, Clerk Superior Court............$	20,374 70	
To amount received of James Pease, Sheriff...	22,807 86	
To amount received of J. McHale, Coroner......	475 86	
		43,658 42
To amount received from tavern licenses........$	3,961 99	
To amount received, tax 1894 and prior........	149,639 21	
To amount received, interest on delinquent taxes....	45,497 50	
		199,098 70
		$ 666,891 83

CR.

By amount credited Salary Fund, 1895.......$	285,715 39	
By amount credited Salary Fund, 1895........	142,739 50	
By amount credited Building Fund, 1895	54,044 22	
By amount credited Miscellaneous Fund, 1895.	58,540 18	
By amount credited Contingent Fund, 1895....	19,757 87	
		$ 560,797 16
By commissions on receipts, ½ per cent on $43,658.42............		218 29

By balance.............		$ 105,876 38
		$ 666,891 83
To balance Dec. 1, 1895..		$ 105,876 38

SALARY FUND, 1895.

DR.

To balance Sept. 2, 1895.		$ 71,681 06
To amount from General Fund account.....		285,715 39
		$ 357,396 45

CR.

By paid orders..........$	325,744 22	
By commissions on disbursements, ½ per cent on $325,744.32.........	1,628 72	$ 327,373 04
By balance.............		30,023 41
		$ 357,396 45
To balance Dec. 1, 1895..		$ 30,023 41
Orders outstanding......		30,023 41

SUPPLY FUND, 1895.

DR.

To balance Sept. 2, 1895.		$ 1,438 01
To amount from General Fund account.........		142,739 50
		$ 144,177 51

CR.

By paid orders..........$	117,867 82	
By commissions on disbursements, ½ per cent on $117,867.82.........	589 34	$ 118,457 16
By balance.............		25,720 35
		$ 144,177 51
To balance Dec. 1, 1895..		$ 25,720 35
Orders outstanding......		25,720 35

BUILDING FUND, 1895.

DR.

To amount received tax 1894.................		$ 5,121 16
To amount from General Fund account.........		54,044 22
		$ 59,165 38

CR.

By paid orders..........$	53,609 08	
By commissions on disbursements, ½ per cent on $55,609.08..........	268 05	$ 53,877 13
By balance.............		5,288 25
		$ 59,165 38
To balance Dec. 1, 1895..		$ 5,288 25
Orders outstanding,.....		5,288 25

MISCELLANEOUS FUND, 1895.

DR.

To balance Sept. 2, 1895.		$ 9,938 72
To amount received tax, 1894.................		3,621 96
To amount from General Fund account.........		$ 58,540 18
		$ 72,100 86

CR.

By paid orders..........$	60,775 09	
By commissions on disbursements, ½ per cent on $60,775.09..........	303 87	$ 61,078 96
By balance.............		11,021 90
		$ 72,100 86
To balance Dec. 1, 1895..		11,021 90
Orders outstanding......		11,021 90

CONTINGENT FUND, 1895.

DR.

To balance Sept. 2, 1895.		$ 458 56
To amount from General Fund account.........		19,757 87
		$ 20,216 43

CR.

By paid orders..........$	19,004 32	
By commissions on disbursements, ½ per cent on $19,004 32..........	95 02	$ 19,099 34
By balance.............		1,117 09
		$ 20,216 43
To balance Dec. 1, 1895..		$ 1,117 09
Orders outstanding......		1,117 09

TUITION FUND.

DR.

To balance Sept. 2, 1895.		$ 2 00
To amount received of O. T. Bright, Co. Supt. of Schools............		2,470 00
		$ 2,472 00

CR.

By paid orders..........		$ 2,135 00
By balance.............		337 00
		$ 2,472 00
To balance Dec 1, 1895,.		$ 337 00
Orders outstanding......		280 00

LIBRARY AND APPARATUS FUND.

DR.

To balance Sept. 2, 1895.		$ 93 14
To amount received of O. T. Bright, Co. Supt. of Schools............		1,000 00
		$ 1,093 14

CR.

By paid orders..........		$ 346 92
By balance.............		746 22
		$ 1,093 14
To balance Dec. 1, 1895..		$ 746 22
Orders outstanding......		62 34

SEMI-ANNUAL REPORT

of D. H. Kochersperger, County Treasurer, of the fees received by him as such Treasurer, and disbursements from same, from June 1, 1895, to December 1, 1895:

TREASURY DEPARTMENT.

COMMISSION ACCOUNT.

DR.

To balance June 1, 1895..		$ 5,095 28
To commissions received since (see exhibit "A")		5,815 42
		$ 10,910 70

CR.

By paid Treasurer's salary..................		$ 2,000 00
By balance		8,910 70
		$ 10,910 70
To balance Dec. 1, 1895..		$ 8,910 70

COLLECTING DEPARTMENT.

COMMISSION ACCOUNT.

DR.

To commissions received (see exhibit "B")		$ 188,740 82

CR.

By amount overdrawn June 1, 1895..........	$ 90,403 83	
By paid clerk hire (see exhibit "C") on account	98,336 99	
		$ 188,740 82

COST ACCOUNT.

DR.

To balance June 1, 1895..		$ 4,874 65
To amount received since (see exhibit "D"......		83,831 37
		$ 88,706 02

CR.

By amount of bill for printing and publishing delinquent tax list June, 1895	$ 42,233 80	
By amount credited County Clerk's fees account for making judgment record	6,010 62	
By amount credited County Clerk's fees account for attending tax sale and issuing tax certificates on account.......	14,000 00	
By paid balance clerk hire (see exhibit "C")......	12,763 80	
		$ 75,008 22
By balance............		13,697 80
		$ 88,706 02
To balance Dec. 1, 1895..		$ 13,697 80

INTEREST ON COUNTY FUNDS.

The following is a statement of the interest received on Cook County funds for the period commencing December 3, 1894, and ending November 30, 1895:

Gross interest received on Cook County funds...		$ 9,647 72

COUNTY CLERK'S FEES ACCOUNT.

DR.

To fees for extending taxes, 1894...........		$ 78,398 80
To fees for making Assessor's books.........		14,733 88
To fees for making judgment record		6,010 62
To fees for attending tax sale and issuing tax certificates on account....		14,000 00
		$ 113,143 30

CR.

By paid Philip Knopf, County Clerk:		
February 25, 1893	$ 10,000 00	
March 5, 1895.........	15,000 00	
March 30, 1895........	15,000 00	
April 30, 1895.........	10,000 00	
June 28, 1895..........	10,000 00	
August 30, 1885.......	10,000 00	
October 1, 1895	10,000 00	
October 30, 1895	10,000 00	
November 30, 1895....	3,132 68	
		$ 93,132 68
By balance.............		20,010 62
		$ 113,143 30
To balance Dec. 1, 1895..		$ 20,010 62

STATE OF ILLINOIS, }
COUNTY OF COOK, } SS.

I, D. H. Kochersperger, Treasurer of said County of Cook, do solemnly swear that the foregoing report is true and correct as therein stated and set forth, according to my best knowledge, information and belief.

D. H. KOCHERSPERGER,
County Treasurer.

Subscribed and sworn to before me this 30th day of December, A. D. 1895.

WILLIAM R. BURCKY,
Notary Public in and for Cook County, Illinois.

NOTE—Statement of interest earned on County funds is this day submitted to you in accordance with the Act concerning Interest on Public Funds, approved June 16, 1893.

D. H. KOCHERSPERGER,
County Treasurer.

REPORT OF COUNTY COLLECTOR.

INTEREST ON DELINQUENT TAXES.

Statement of the account of D. H. Kochersperger, County Collector, for County tax and interest on delinquent taxes for the year 1894:

DR.		
To tax 1894, on real and personal property	$2,120,684 52	
To tax 1893, and prior years on warrant, 1894	2,714 93	
		$2,123,399 45
To tax 1894, paid by different claimants		23 74
To tax 1893, and prior, collected, not on warrant of 1894		1,852 43
To interest collected on delinquent taxes under Sec. 177 of Revised Statutes		110,147 51
		$2,235,423 13

CR.		
By tax 1894, forfeited to State	$ 1,462 22	
By tax 1894, judgment refused	4,309 59	
By tax 1894, errors	506 07	
By tax 1894, uncollected on personal property, insolvencies, removals, etc.	33,225 88	
By tax 1893 and prior years uncollected	2,376 32	
		$ 41,880 08
By commissions paid to town collectors, 2 per cent on $657,235.49	$ 13,144 72	
By County Collector's commission, ¾ per cent on $644,090.77, received town collectors	4,830 68	
By County Collector's commissions, 1½ per cent on $1,426,160.05, collected by County Collector	21,392 40	
		$ 39,367 80
By amount paid into County Treasury—		
January	$ 46,554 64	
February	100,000 00	
March	420,000 00	
April	649,090 77	
May	457,865 61	
June	80,369 85	
July	95,717 08	
August	100,697 47	
September	67,557 93	
October	76,120 40	
November	60,201 50	
		2,154,175 25
		$2,235,423 13

COOK COUNTY RECORDER.

From the earliest history of the human family it has been the ambition of mankind to acquire land. Once acquired and a home established, the true man will fight until his last drop of blood has been drunk by the soil in order to protect it. Such being the importance of the ownership of real estate, it is but natural that great care is used to prevent the possibility of its loss. Among all the laws of this or any other civilized country where a good government exists, those relating to matters of realty have ever been the most carefully provided, and the laws in regard to the recording of papers which affect land are the most important in the statutes for the reason that all such instruments must be recorded to make them legal.

The Recorder's office, then, by reason of the generally accepted value of realty, is without any doubt the most important department of a municipal government. Chicago, large as she is, and great as she is, is still but an infant in maturity as compared with many of the other large cities of this country or of the old world, and yet the Recorder's office of Cook County is the most extensive, the most complete and the most ably conducted of any such County institution in the world. The reasons for this are so apparent to any one who will take the pains to look into the matter, that no doubt of the truth of the statement can be harbored in the mind of any one for a minute. Chicago has leaped into the second position as regards size with such phenomenal rapidity that her sisters look upon her in wonder, and while those which have been outstripped in the race, grudgingly admit her greatness, and the one which still outnumbers her in population trembles for its laurels, they all acknowledge her as the eighth wonder of the world.

While Chicago has grown rapidly and steadily her real estate has been more a matter of speculation than could be possible in an old and thoroughly established city. It was but a few years ago that all of the city was embraced within some half dozen of her present blocks, having the site of the County building for a common center. Year by year she has radiated out until today one of her streets extends in a straight line for nearly twenty-five miles without going beyond the city limits, and her total area reaches nearly 200 square miles.

This constant extension indicates frequent purchases of land, and these purchases all mean business for the office of the Recorder.

Although this institution was established some time before the fire, that terrible calamity destroyed all records, and the office, as it is today, practically dates from the time of the great conflagration. And a proud record it has made. Over 5,500 books are there to be found, and as each book contains 500 pages it shows that at least 2,750,000 instruments have been filed since the fire. The filing cases in this office are all fire proof and are of the latest improved pattern, they being the product of the Fenton Metallic Mfg. Co. of Jamestown, N. Y., who have in the main furnished Cook County with their filing and book cases.

To do the work of this office requires a great many hands and the list of employes now foots up to 225. This force is rather larger than it was under past administrations, but the enlargement has been made necessary by the increase of documents to be filed, and also by the necessity of getting the work done with more expedition than formerly. It used to take three weeks to put a single instrument through the various rooms, whereas now, under the improved system, and with the increased force, it is done in ten days' time.

As will be seen, it is matters of real estate that constitute the bulk of the work of the Recorder's office, but it also has to deal with the mortgages of personal property, and some faint idea of what the amount of labor is, may be had when it is stated that one man often enters one hundred instruments a day for filing.

The papers of all kinds filed in 1895 amounted to 173,782. Nothing is ever filed in this office that is in any way obscene. The different classes of instruments this department has to deal with embraces bills of sale, tax deeds, warrantee deeds, trust claim deeds, trust deeds, releases, mortgages, chattel mortgages, charters, voluntary assignments.

Of course there are some slack days. The weather affects the business of this office very materially, as when it is storming or cold people do not go out to look at property, and the consequence is the sales are light and the clerks get a breathing spell. As high as $1,650 has been received in this office in one day, and when it is considered that the fees are none of them large for the work done, it will be admitted that at times it taxes energies of the 225 employes to get through with the duties. There are two windows, the "Receiving" and "Delivery," through which the business of the recording office is transacted, with two clerks at the first and four at the second. The abstract business is an important feature, as the law requires that at any time the public may ask for an abstract of title. This work has greatly increased since the decision of the Supreme Court making abstracts from this department merchantable. The vaults, too, where the public are permitted to examine the books, necessitates the attendance of many clerks.

All the business of the Recorder's office is done in different departments which, outside of the Recorder himself, number eight. Samuel B. Chase is the Recorder. Under him are W. C. Niehoff, in charge of the receiving and delivery department; Theodore Nelson, chief deputy; A. L. Brown, cashier; Julius Ludwig, superintendent folio department; P. A. Hines, superintendent abstract department; M. P. Hartney, superintendent vault department; H. L. Herbert, superintendent map department; J. L. Cochran, receiving clerk, and Daniel Degan, delivery clerk.

It may be of interest to many to know the inside workings of a well-managed and complete Recorder's office. In the first place it should be understood that all papers connected with real estate or personal property must be recorded. In following, say a deed, through its course before it is ready for delivery it will have to go first to the receiving clerk, who numbers and dates it with the day of the month, the day of the week and the hour it is received. From there the deed goes to the original entry clerk, in same room, in whose book are entered the names of both the grantor and the grantee. The next move is to the grantor book and then to the grantee book. These books are alphabetically indexed and are for the general convenience of the public. After this the instrument goes to Room 11, where tract index sheets are made, and then to Room 28 to be compared with the tract index sheets by the comparers. From here to Room 10 it goes and is there put in the hands of a clerk to distribute to the folio writers. Before leaving this room the instrument is compared with the folio writer's work and is then charged to the delivery department in Room 7 in a numbered book especially kept for that purpose. Then back to Room 7 the instrument is taken for the signature of the Recorder and to be entered in a special book known under the name of "book and paging." This is a book which gives the number and page of other books. Then the distribution is made to alphabetically arranged boxes.

One of the features of this department is the box system. These small compartments are rented to regular customers of the Recorder's office in order to facilitate the work. The papers passing through the department are put in these customer boxes, if they have one, and are charged to that box as well as the individual. This system saves a great amount of trouble, both on the part of the office and the customer. When it is called for it is charged to the party in the delivery book.

The endeavor is made to get as many checks on an instrument as possible, not only to avoid mistakes but to detect them if made. If an error is discovered a postal card is sent to the interested party notifying him of the fact. This is purely a gratuitous act, no law of the department requiring it to be done.

The work of the department is somewhat facilitated by having in the books printed blanks for the ordinary statutory documents which only need to be filled in.

The map department is one of the principal features of this office, and it is here that property is first platted, and the map department of the County Clerk's office take their maps from the office of the records. The greatest care possible is taken to prevent the recording of forgeries, and as a protection against the danger of unscrupulous people making changes in entries in the books, no one is allowed to take a pen and ink into the vaults.

The Recorder's office in this County affords a revenue to the County instead of being an expense. It is more than self supporting, and under the able management of Recorder Chase and the heads of the various departments it constantly grows in usefulness. Under the present management it is certainly a pleasure to do business there, as expedition is made a feature and courtesy and polite attention are met with on every hand.

Below are the two semi-annual financial reports of Recorder Chase for 1895:

FIFTH SEMI-ANNUAL REPORT

of Samuel B. Chase, Recorder of Cook County, from December 1, 1894, to May 31 1895:

Total receipts for recording documents Nos. 2,140,932 to 2,227,706, both inclusive, making 86,775 documents.....$	85,419 10	
Total receipts for certified copies...............	1,195 60	
Grand total..........		$ 86,614 70

DISBURSEMENTS.

Deficit December 1, 1894.$	2,930 77	

PAY ROLL FOR CLERKS.

December ....$	7,231 44	
January	7,389 77	
February	7,121 47	
March..................	7,114 18	
April..................	7,233 95	
May....................	7,396 43	
	—$	46,418 01

PAY ROLL FOR FOLIO-WRITERS.

December ....$	5,704 22	
January	5,534 17	
February	4,133 90	
March..................	5,554 56	
April	5,979 49	
May....................	6,375 80	
	—$	33,282 14
Samuel B. Chase, salary.$	2,500 00	
		2,500 00

ABSTRACT DEPARTMENT.

Total receipts from December 1, 1894, to May 31, 1895	$	4,627 20

DISBURSEMENTS.

PAY ROLL ABSTRACT DEPARTMENT.

December ....$	1,082 48	
January	1,082 48	
February	1,082 48	
March..................	1,082 48	
April	1,038 56	
May....................	1,082 48	
	—$	6,450 96

PAY ROLL FOLIO-WRITERS—ABSTRACT DEP'T.

December .... $	77 76	
January	51 87	
February	71 27	
March..................	85 23	
April..................	39 25	
May....................	67 22	
	—$	392 60

To be charged to Special Appropriation of $2,500.00 for comparing and re-writing Tract book.

December ....$	509 50	
January	230 50	
February	258 34	
March..................	424 84	
April..................	198 09	
May....................	228 50	
	—$	1,849 77
Samuel B. Chase, salary.		500 00

RECAPITULATION.

Total receipts Recording Department..........	$	86,614 70
Total receipts Abstract Department		4,627 25
Total receipts box rents.		2,117 20

SIXTH SEMI-ANNUAL REPORT

of Samuel B. Chase, Recorder of Deeds of Cook County, from June 1, 1895, to November 30, 1895:

RECAPITULATION.

Total Receipts Recording Department		$ 87,256 50	
Total Receipts, Abstract Department		6,018 05	
TOTAL DISBURSEMENTS.			
Pay Rolls, Recording Department	$ 44,028 38		
Pay Rolls, Folio Department	35,073 49		
Pay Rolls, Abstract Department	$ 6,369 88		
Pay Rolls, Abstract Folio Department	664 59		
Pay Rolls, Special Appropriation	657 67		
Samuel B. Chase, salary	3,000 00		
Balance to Credit of Cook County	3,480 54		
	$ 93,274 55	$ 93,274 55	

THE NEW COOK COUNTY JAIL.

From a humanitarian point of view it is doubtless unfortunate that such things as jails are necessary. But they are necessary and they have been from the earliest days of mankind. Being, then, a needful adjunct of social conditions, it becomes advisable to have such institutions built and arranged on the best possible plans. To do this it is necessary to have a man at the helm who knows his business and who has made a study of the needs of human frailty in this line.

For this vicinity, for the County of Cook, such a man was found in County Commissioner Thomas J. McNichols. He was brought into prominence by the excellent ideas he advanced and the energy with which he pushed the scheme of having the water mains conducted to the county institution at Dunning. It is acknowledged to be a fact that no other feature in connection with this establishment has been so beneficial or has contributed so much to ameliorate the condition of the afflicted consigned there. If anything else were needed to prove its value, the recent fire in the laundry at this institution should be sufficient. The fact that there was plenty of water at hand with which to fight the fire went a long way in saving the institutions from a total loss, and not only saved the tax payers of Cook County from financial loss, but saved the inmates from much suffering. This was all the result of the labors of Mr. McNichols, who, with it almost seems a prophetic eye, saw the calamity coming and inaugurated the plan of salvation.

Mr. McNichols was made chairman of the building committee for the county buildings, and no better choice could have been made in consideration of the fact that a new jail was in contemplation. Mr. McNichols was the right man in the right place, for he had made a study of the business and he knew just what was wanted.

Long ago it had been recognized as a fact that the old jail in Chicago was very far from meeting its requirements and that a new building was necessary. At a meeting of the Board of County Commissioners, held in January, 1895, the following resolution was passed :

"WHEREAS, The building now occupied as a jail is wholly inadequate for the use of the county, and is a constant menace to the lives and health of the prisoners, as well as the officers and guards employed there. Prisoners with dangerous and contagious diseases are confined in the same cell with well persons, and the conditions are such as should not exist in any civilized community."

Much followed this, but all to the effect that a new jail was needed. The resolution was adopted and the next move was to secure a plan for the institution. The county architect and the superintendent of public service were instructed to advertise for bids. Finally these bids were opened and among the successful bidders were Edward J. Molloy, E. Heldmaier & Co., August Zander Company, James A. Miller & Bro., and the Evans Marble Co.

Edward J. Molloy had the contract for the masonry work. The reputation of Mr. Molloy is well known, and the excellence of his methods was never more clearly shown than in the foundations and walls he put up for this new jail. Without completion, without a roof, or, for that matter, without anything like an adequate protection, the walls and foundations have stood all winter without settling in the least. This, in Chicago, where rock bottom is so far to reach, can only be expressed as the work of an expert.

There is no feature of any building which attracts so much attention as the stone work. E. Heldmaier & Co. have in this line achieved a great reputation, and it has only been increased by what they have done in connection with the new jail.

In the construction of a building there are many things of importance which do not show on the surface. One of these features is the lathing and plastering. This work was entrusted to the August Zander Company, and these people used both the Turnbull & Cullerton steel lath and the Monarch fire-proof lath, manufactured by the Nowak Construction Company. This material has been found to be admirable for the purpose, and is not only a great credit to the inventor, but to the contractors who use it.

The roof of any building is as important a feature as any other part. James A. Miller & Bro. have made a study of this, and their roofing and sheet metal work has attracted the attention of builders all over the country.

There is no reason why even an institution for the confinement of criminals should not be to a certain extent embellished. While it is not necessary nor desirable that this feature should prevail to the same extent as in a private residence, there is no reason why it should be entirely excluded from the plans of such a building as the Cook County Jail. It was for this reason that the Evans Marble Company were given the contract for the decorative mosaic work in this building. It was the excellence of their work in other places which secured for them this contract. It goes without saying that such a firm, with a good reputation to sustain, would not fail to do themselves credit in a contract on so important a building as the Cook County Jail.

SALARY APPROPRIATIONS FOR 1896.

One of the important and interesting features in connection with the County Institutions is the number of employes, their duties and the salary each one receives. This is particularly interesting matter to the public, and it is the duty of every tax payer to make a study of it, as it is from his pocket the money comes.

Below is a table showing practically the salaries of Cook County Institutions, for 1896:

COUNTY HOSPITAL.	Salaries per year.
1 warden .... $	2,500 00
1 chief clerk	1,500 00
1 bookkeeper	900 00
2 receiving clerks	1,200 00
1 night clerk	600 00
1 night supervisor	600 00
1 registrar	900 00
1 custodian	720 00
1 druggist	900 00
1 assistant druggist	720 00
1 druggist's helper	360 00
2 custodians of instruments	720 00
2 housekeepers	960 00
1 head painter	636 00
3 painters	1,620 00
2 carpenters	1,272 00
1 mattress maker	480 00
1 storekeeper	720 00
1 baker	600 00
1 assistant baker	480 00
1 cook	660 00
1 cook	600 00
1 assistant cook	300 00
1 cook, night .... $	360 00
1 butcher	480 00
4 car men	1,440 00
1 gardener	540 00
1 laundryman	420 00
3 assistant laundrymen	720 00
1 bathroom clerk, male	360 00
1 bathroom clerk, female	300 00
1 barn foreman	420 00
3 teamsters	1,080 00
1 ambulance man	240 00
1 undertaker	360 00
1 assistant undertaker	300 00
1 coffin maker	480 00
1 morgue keeper	360 00
1 weigher	600 00
1 head porter	360 00
6 porters	1,800 00
3 doorkeepers	1,080 00
2 watchmen	600 00
2 laborers	720 00
1 janitor	300 00
7 window cleaners	1,680 00
1 fumigator	240 00

	Salaries per year.
2 messengers	$ 480 00
1 chief engineer	1,200 00
3 assistant engineers	2,160,00
2 electric engineers	1,440 00
3 firemen	1,440 00
3 firemen, 6 months	720 00
3 coal and ash wheelers	1,080 00
3 coal and ash wheelers, 6 months...	540 00
1 boiler washer	360 00
1 steamfitter	792 00
1 assistant steamfitter	480 00
1 plumber	792 00
1 assistant plumber	480 00
1 sewer man	360 00
3 elevator men	1,440 00
1 head seamstress	300 00
2 sewing machine women	432 00
3 linen room women	648 00
1 laundress	240 00
2 wash room women	432 00
2 dry room women	432 00
1 head ironer	300 00
2 shirt ironers	432 00
9 ironers	1,620 00
4 manglers	720 00
30 scrubwomen	6,480 00
1 head waitress	240 00
6 waitresses	1,296 00
3 chambermaids	540 00
1 woman, to help baker	180 00
3 tin washers	648 00
4 nurses	1,200 00
3 nurses	720 00
Illinois Training School for Nurses, nursing in Wards 1, 2, 3, 4, 5, 6, 7, 8, 9, 10, 13, 14, 20, 22 and 24, and Contageous Diseases Ward, including all special nursing	200 00

DETENTION HOSPITAL.

1 county physician	$ 2,000 00
1 assistant county physician	900 00
1 clerk	720 00
1 matron	420 00
1 janitor	540 00
6 attendants, male	1,800 00
6 attendants, female	1,800 00
3 attendants, children's ward	900 00
1 cook	360 00
1 assistant cook	240 00
2 waitresses	384 00
1 scrub woman	216 00
Salaries for Hospital and Detention Hospital	$ 98,292 00

GENERAL SUPERINTENDENT AT DUNNING.

1 general superintendent	$ 2,500 00
1 chief clerk	1,200 00
1 chief engineer	1,200 00
1 general bookkeeper and storekeeper	900 00
1 assistant storekeeper	420 00
1 assistant storekeeper	360 00
1 stenographer	300 00
1 druggist	720 00
1 assistant druggist	480 00
2 steamfitters	1,584 00
2 helpers	720 00
2 plumbers	1,584 00
2 helpers	720 00
1 head painter	636 00
1 gardener	540 00
1 assistant gardener	360 00
1 mason and plasterer	$ 720 00
1 electrician	480 00
2 carpenters	1,272 00
1 butcher	600 00
1 helper	300 00
1 mattressmaker	420 00
2 helpers	360 00
2 tinsmiths	600 00
1 assistant painter, for six months ...	300 00
1 glazier and repairer	300 00
1 calciminer	420 00
1 teamster	300 00
1 telephone messenger	216 00
1 driver	120 00
1 bus driver	120 00
	$ 20,752 00

1 physician (male)	$ 1,200 00
1 assistant physician (male)	600 00
1 physician (female)	1,200 00
1 assistant physician (female)	600 00
3 assistant engineers	2,160 00
3 firemen	1,440 00
3 firemen for five months	600 00
1 supervisor	720 00
1 assistant supervisor	360 00
1 supervisoress	480 00
1 assistant supervisoress	360 00
1 housekeeper	480 00
1 assistant housekeeper	360 00
1 first cook	660 00
1 second cook	600 00
1 third cook	300 00
1 night cook	240 00
1 first baker	600 00
1 second baker	480 00
2 car men	600 00
1 laundryman	420 00
1 assistant laundryman	300 00
1 laundress	300 00
3 assistant laundresses	648 00
1 seamstress	360 00
3 assistant seamstresses	720 00
1 assistant, steam kitchen	300 00
1 general repairer	360 00
1 outside night watchman	300 00
88 attendants	31,680 00
6 dining room girls	1,152 00
1 tailor	360 00
1 bath room man	360 00
1 marker	360 00
1 furniture repairer	360 00
1 outside foreman	360 00
1 inside foreman	360 00
1 lawn man	360 00
1 day police	360 00
	$ 53,460 00

POOR HOUSE.

1 physician (male)	$ 1,200 00
1 assistant physician	600 00
1 physician, female	1,200 00
1 supervisor	720 00
1 supervisoress	480 00
1 housekeeper	480 00
1 general office clerk and time keeper	900 00
3 assistant engineers	2,160 00
3 firemen	1,440 00
1 general repairer	360 00
1 tailor	360 00
1 seamstress	360 00

	Salaries per year.
1 assistant seamstress	$ 240 00
1 janitress	240 00
1 bath-room man	360 00
2 dining-room girls	384 00
1 laundryman	420 00
1 laundress	300 00
1 assistant laundress	216 00
1 first baker	600 00
1 second baker	480 00
1 first cook	660 00
1 second cook	600 00
1 cooks' helper	300 00
3 nurses	900 00
17 nurses	4,080 00
6 watchmen	1,800 00
1 farmer	600 00
1 assistant farmer	300 00
3 farm hands, when required	720 00
1 yard man	300 00
1 outside night watchman	300 00
1 telephone messenger	216 00
1 pig-pen man	120 00
	$ 24,396 00

PAY OF NURSES.

And it is directed that the nurses in the Poor House be paid $18.00 per month for the first three months of service, $20.00 per month for the second three months of service, and the amount so appropriated thereafter; and that attendants in Insane Asylum be paid $20 00 per month for the first three months, $25.00 per month for the second three months, and $30.00 per month thereafter, and that the General Superintendent designate on his pay-roll the length of time attendeuts have been in service of the County.

TOTAL SALARIES.

General Superintendent	$ 20,752 00
Insane Asylum	53,460 00
Poor House	24,396 00
Total	$ 98,608 00

COUNTY AGENT'S OFFICE.

1 county agent	$ 2,000 00
1 assistant county agent	1,500 00
1 secretary	1,200 00
1 clerk branch office	1,200 00
1 bookkeeper	1,200 00
1 out-put man	1,200 00
1 night watchman	540 00
Necessary visitors and clerks (to be determined by order of Board), $3.00 per day	10,000 00
10 physicians, (they to furnish medicine)	4,200 00
	$ 23,040 00

CUSTODIAN AND COUNTY EMPLOYES—COURT HOUSE.

1 custodian	$ 1,800 00
1 clerk	900 00
8 elevator men	7,200 00
12 watchmen	9,360 00
16 janitors	11,520 00
4 window cleaners	2,880 00
20 janitresses	10,800 00
1 chief engineer	1,500 00
3 assistant engineers	2,700 00
5 firemen	3,600 00
1 fireman (6 months)	360 00
1 pumpman	720 00
2 carpenters	$ 1,800 00
1 coal passer	720 00
1 plumber	1,020 00
1 steam fitter at Court House and Criminal Court	1,000 00
	$ 57,880 00

CUSTODIAN AND COUNTY EMPLOYES—CRIMINAL COURT BUILDING.

1 custodian	$ 1,800 00
4 elevator men	3,600 00
8 watchmen	6,240 00
11 janitors	7,920 00
2 window cleaners	1,440 00
15 janitresses	8,100 00
1 chief engineer	1,500 00
3 assistant engineers	2,700 00
5 firemen	3,600 00
1 fireman, 6 months	360 00
1 pumpman	720 00
2 carpenters	1,800 00
1 plumber	1,020 00
1 coal passer	720 00
	$ 41,520 00

SHERIFF'S OFFICE.

1 chief deputy	$ 3,600 00
1 chief clerk	2,500 00
1 jailer	2,000 00
2 assistant jailers	3,000 00
30 deputies	60,000 00
1 real estate clerk	1,800 00
1 execution clerk	1,800 00
1 summons clerk	1,800 00
1 assistant summons clerk	1,200 00
1 general clerk	1,200 00
5 office clerks	5,000 00
1 jail clerk	1,500 00
1 assistant jail clerk	1,000 00
95 bailiffs	119,700 00
34 jail guards	34,000 00
1 typewriter	720 00
1 messenger	720 00
1 office watchman	780 00
3 matrons in jail	1,800 00
1 laundress	480 00
2 elevator men, for new elevators at Criminal Court, carrying prisoners	1,800 00
	$ 246,400 00

OFFICE SUPERINTENDENT OF PUBLIC SERVICE.

1 superintendent of public service	$ 4,000 00
1 chief clerk	2,000 00
1 auditor	1,800 00
1 bookkeeper	1,500 00
1 assistant bookkeeper	1,200 00
1 secretary	1,500 00
1 clerk and buyer	1,500 00
1 messenger	720 00
1 typewriter	720 00
1 foreman of repairs	1,200 00
	$ 16,140 00

COUNTY BOARD.

1 county commissioner, president Board	$ 4,700 00
14 county commissioners	42,000 00
1 committee clerk	2,500 00
1 county electrician	1,200 00
1 chief jury clerk	1,200 00
2 assistant jury clerks	1,800 00
	$ 52,900 00

COMPTROLLER'S OFFICE AND CLERK OF THE BOARD OF COUNTY COMMISSIONERS.

	Salaries per year.
1 Deputy Comptroller and Clerk of County Board	$ 3,600 00
1 chief clerk and bookkeeper	2,500 00
1 minute clerk and record writer	2,000 00
1 bill clerk	2,000 00
1 cashier	1,500 00
1 assistant bookkeeper and general clerk	1,500 00
1 comptroller's clerk	1,350 00
1 janitress	540 00
	$ 14,990 00

OFFICE OF STATE'S ATTORNEY.

1 state's attorney	$ 6,600 00
2 assistants	8,000 00
1 assistant	3,000 00
2 assistants	4,800 00
4 assistants	7,200 00
Stenography and typewriting work	7,500 00
Extra help, when required, provided the salary of no one person shall exceed $250.00 per month	5,300 00
	$ 42,400 00

OFFICE OF THE COUNTY ATTORNEY.

1 County Attorney	$ 4,000 00
1 First Assistant County Attorney	1,800 00
1 Second Assistant County Attorney	1,800 00
1 assistant and clerk	1,200 00
1 stenographer	600 00
	$ 9,400 00

OFFICE OF THE COUNTY SUPERINTENDENT OF SCHOOLS.

2 assistant superintendents	$ 4,000 00
1 clerk	900 00
	$ 4,900 00

CLERK OF THE CRIMINAL COURT.

1 chief clerk	$ 2,500 00
1 assistant chief clerk	1,800 00
3 record writers	5 400 00
1 general record writer	1,800 00
1 fee and process clerk	1,500 00
4 court clerks	4,800 00
1 platter and officer clerk	1,500 00
1 cashier and quasi-criminal record writer	1,500 00
7 office clerks	8,400 00
5 general clerks	5,000 00
1 judgment clerk	1,200 00
2 execution clerks	3,000 00
1 indictment record writer	1,000 00
2 vault clerks	2 000 00
1 assistant record writer	1,500 00
1 bond clerk	1,200 00
1 venire clerk	1,000 00
1 docket clerk	1,000 00
1 messenger and stenographer	900 00
	$ 47,000 00

ELECTION COMMISSIONERS.

3 election commissioners	$ 4,500 00
1 chief clerk	3,500 00
Election purposes	70,000 00
	$ 78,000 00

CIVIL SERVICE COMMISSION.

3 civil service commissioners	$ 4,500 00

SUMMARY.

	Salaries.
Hospital and Detention Hospital	$ 98,292 00
General Superintendent of County Institutions, Dunning	20,752 00
Insane Asylum	53,460 00
Poor House and Poor Farm	24,396 00
County Agent	23,040 00
Custodian Court House	57,880 00
Custodian Criminal Court	41,520 00
Sheriff	246,400 00
Superintendent Public Service	16,140 00
County Board and Jury clerks	52,900 00
Comptroller	14,990 00
State's Attorney	42,400 00
County Attorney	9,400 00
County Superintendent of Schools	4,900 00
Clerk Criminal Court	47,000 00
Election Commissioners	78,000 00
Civil Service Commission	4,500 00
County Clerk	....
County Treasurer	....
Recorder	....
Recorder, Torrens Land System Department	....
Clerk Circuit Court	....
Clerk Superior Court	....
Clerk Probate Court	....
Coroner	....
	$ 835,970 00

COUNTY TREASURER'S OFFICE.

1 Assistant Treasurer	$ 4,000 00
1 cashier	2,400 00
1 assistant cashier	1,800 00
1 bookkeeper	3,600 00
1 assistant bookkeeper	1,800 00
1 assistant bookkeeper	1,500 00
1 chief clerk	2,500 00
1 assistant chief clerk	2,000 00
3 receiving tellers	5,400 00
3 clerks, first grade	4,950 00
3 clerks, second grade	4,320 00
1 stenographer	1,200 00
1 messenger	720 00
2 day watchmen	1,560 00
2 night watchmen	1,560 00
1 draughtsman	1,500 00
1 assistant draughtsman	1,200 00
1 mail clerk	1,500 00

FOR EIGHT MONTHS.

4 assistant chief clerks	$ 4,320 00
2 receiving tellers	2,400 00
15 clerks, first grade	15,600 00
20 clerks, second grade	18,400 00
10 messengers (cash clerks)	3,600 00

EXTRA MEN BY THE DAY.

75 men to be employed as required ($3.00 to $4.00 per day)	$ 93,900 00

NIGHT AND SUNDAY WORK.

During the month of March, 25 men	$ 2,600 00
During the month of April, 60 men	6,240 00
During the month of May, 60 men	6,480 00
During the month of June, 15 men	1,500 00
During the month of July, 15 men	1,620 00
During the month of August, 15 men	1,620 00
During the month of September, 5 men	500 00
During the month of October, 5 men	540 00
	$ 202,830 00

COUNTY CLERK'S OFFICE.

	Salaries per year.
1 chief deputy.......................$	3,000 00
1 cashier..........................	2,000 00
1 bookkeeper......................	2,000 00
1 deputy, redemption department....	1,800 00
7 assistant deputies, redemption department........................	10,500 00
1 deputy, tax sales..................	1,500 00
1 deputy, tax extension............	2,000 00
1 assistant deputy, tax extension....	1,650 00
1 assistant deputy, tax extension and railroad tax	1,500 00
1 railroad warrant clerk............	1,500 00
1 deputy, marriage license	1,500 00
1 assistant deputy, marriage license..	1,200 00
1 deputy, vital statistics............	1,200 00
1 assistant deputy, vital statistics....	1,200 00
1 map clerk........................	1,650 00
3 assistant map clerks	3,600 00
1 vault clerk, 1st	1,200 00
1 vault clerk, 2d..................	900 00
1 vault clerk, books and papers	1,500 00
1 stenographer	1,200 00
1 watchman, day..................	720 00
1 watchman, night................	840 00
107 extra men on tax extension, special assessments and tax sales, etc., at $3 to $4 per day, according to qualification....................	133,964 00
1 general man on tax extension, special assessments and tax sales at $125 per month, $1,500 per year. (This amount to be taken from the appropriation of 107 extra men.)	

CLERK OF COUNTY COURT.

1 chief clerk.......................$	2,500 00
1 assistant chief clerk..............	1,650 00
1 record writer......................	1,800 00
1 record writer, special assessments..	1,800 00
1 process clerk	1,600 00
1 minute clerk	1,410 00
1 minute clerk	1,410 00
10 extra men on special assessment work at $3 and $4 per day.......	12,520 00
1 general man on special assessment work at $125 per month, $1,500 per year. (This amount to be paid from the appropriation of 10 extra men.)	
Salaries for County Clerk and Clerk of County Court................$	202,814 00

CLERK OF CIRCUIT COURT.

1 chief clerk.......................$	2,500 00
1 bookkeeper and cashier...........	2,400 00
2 execution clerks..................	3,600 00
3 common law record writers.... ...	5,400 00
1 assistant law record writer	1,500 00
4 chancery record writers...........	7,200 00
1 judgment record writer	1,650 00
4 decree record writers.............	6,000 00
1 condemnation record writer	1,500 00
1 recording clerk..................	1,500 00
7 common law minute clerks........	9,240 00
1 vault clerk	900 00
8 general clerks	9,600 00
14 office clerks	14,000 00
2 transcript clerks.................	2,400 00
1 lien docket clerk.................	1,500 00
For extra help for records and transcripts $4 per day...............	2,500 00
$	73,390 00

CLERK OF SUPERIOR COURT.

	Salaries per year.
1 chief clerk ....$	2,500 00
1 bookkeeper and cashier...........	2,400 00
2 execution clerks..................	3,600 00
3 law record writers	5,400 00
1 assistant law record writer.........	1,500 00
2 chancery minute clerks and record writers.........................	3,600 00
1 judgment record writer	1,650 00
2 decree record writers..............	3,000 00
1 condemnation record writer.......	1,500 00
1 recording clerk..................	1,500 00
6 common law minute clerks........	7,920 00
1 vault and file clerk..............	1,000 00
10 office clerks.....................	10,000 00
6 general clerks....................	7,200 00
Extra help for folio work, etc., as required, not exceeding in the aggregate 625 days' work..........	2,500 00
$	55,270 00

CLERK OF PROBATE COURT.

3 assistants to Judge...............$	7,500 00
1 chief clerk	2,500 00
1 cashier..........................	1,800 00
5 record writers	9,000 00
1 fee and process clerk	1,800 00
1 entry clerk.......................	1,800 00
1 general clerk	1,600 00
2 docket clerks....................	2,640 00
1 claim clerk......................	1,200 00
1 citation clerk....................	1,400 00
1 transcript clerk..................	1,400 00
1 comparer.........................	1,400 00
10 clerks, $3.00 to $4.00 per day	12,536 00
6 recording warrant and appraisement clerks.........................	6,600 00
1 file clerk........................	1,200 00
2 file clerks	2,200 00
3 clerks	3,000 00
1 stenographer	1,200 00
2 general clerks....................	2,400 00
$	63,176 00

CORONER'S OFFICE.

1 Coroner..........................$	5,000 00
1 chief deputy	2,500 00
1 deputy and physician............	2,000 00
9 deputy coroners	13,500 00
1 clerk............................	1,200 00
1 clerk at morgue	900 00
1 morgue keeper	600 00
1 assistant morgue keeper...........	360 00
$	26,060 00

RECORDER'S OFFICE.

1 chief deputy ....$	2,500 00
1 superintendent, folio department...	1,800 00
1 assistant superintendent, folio department.......................	1,100 00
1 chief comparer, folio department..	1,500 00
18 comparers, folio department......	18,000 00
1 bookkeeper and cashier...........	1,800 00
1 receiving clerk...................	1,650 00
1 assistant receiving clerk..........	1,200 00
1 delivery clerk	1,400 00
1 assistant delivery clerk...........	1,200 00
2 box and distributing clerks........	2,200 00
1 original entry clerk..............	1,500 00
2 assistant original entry clerks	2,400 00
1 grantor index clerk........	1,500 00
1 assistant grantor index clerk	1,200 00

	Salaries per year.
1 grantee index clerk	$ 1,500 00
1 assistant grantee index clerk	1,200 00
1 chattel index clerk	1,200 00
3 book and paging clerks	3,300 00
1 book clerk	1,000 00
1 book clerk	900 00
1 draughtsman and map clerk	1,400 00
3 assistant map clerks	3,600 00
1 superintendent, examining and vault department	1,500 00
1 vault clerk	1,000 00
1 vault clerk	900 00
1 examining clerk	1,200 00
1 superintendent track indices	1,650 00
1 assistant superintendent track indices	1,320 00
1 track index poster	1,200 00
5 assistant track index posters	5,500 00
3 original sheet track index clerks	3 300 00
1 original sheet track index comparer	1,200 00
1 reviser re-transcribed indices	1,500 00
1 assistant reviser re-transcribed indices	1,100 00
8 re-transcribing clerks	8,800 00
1 watchman	780 00
1 janitress	540 00
1 messenger	600 00
1 superintendent abstract department	1,650 00
2 abstract makers	3,000 00
2 assistant abstract makers	2,200 00
1 tax clerk	1,320 00
1 judgment clerk, courts	1,320 00
1 assistant judgment clerk	1,200 00
1 judgment clerk, office	1,200 00
1 assistant judgment clerk, office	1,100 00
3 scrub women	1,620 00
Folio writers, 4½ cents per folio for regular folio work and 5 cents when comparing	75,000 00
For comparing, perfecting and re-writing track books	2,500 00
	$ 179,250 00

ADDITIONAL HELP ALLOWED BY ORDER OF COURT FOR TORRENS LAND SYSTEM.

The following to be paid out of the actual receipts in the registrar's office, and in no case shall the amount paid for salaries exceed the actual receipts in this department.

Estimated receipts by ex-officio Registrar, Registrar Department...... $ 42,500 00

$31,750 of the actual receipts is appropriated for salaries as follows:

	Salaries per year.
3 examiners (attorneys)	$ 15,000 00
1 chief deputy	1,500 00
1 register and application clerk	1,500 00
1 cashier	750 00
2 chainmen	3,000 00
1 judgment clerk	1,300 00
1 assistant judgment clerk	1,200 00
1 track index clerk	1,300 00
1 alphabetical and transfer clerk	1,300 00
1 keeper of vault	1,200 00
1 publication clerk	1,200 00
1 inspector of premises	1,200 00
1 tax and special assessment clerk	1,300 00
	$ 31,750 00

SUMMARY OF ESTIMATES OF RESOURCES OUTSIDE OF TAX LEVY, AND SALARIES TO BE PAID THEREFROM.

	Estimate of receipts.	Estimate of salaries.
Jurors and witness fees, etc.		$ 225,000 00
Salaries Judges of all Courts of Record		112,000 00
County Treasurer's office	$ 330,000 00	202,830 00
Recorder's office	180,000 00	179,250 00
Registrar department	42,500 00	31,750 00
County Clerk's office and Clerk County Court	220,000 00	202,814 00
Clerk of Circuit Court	170,000 00	73,390 00
Clerk of Superior Court	100,000 00	55,270 00
Clerk of Probate Court	100,000 00	63,176 00
Coroner	1,000 00	26,060 00
Clerk of Criminal Court	1,000 00	....
Sheriff	50,000 00	....
	$1,194,500 00	$1,171,540 00

INDEX.

INDEX TO ILLUSTRATIONS.

INDEX TO ADVERTISEMENTS.

EDWARD J. MOLLOY.

General Contractor for All Kinds of Public Buildings

218 Builders and Traders Exchange, Chicago.

Among the recent public buildings erected by Mr. Molloy, the new Cook County Jail (which is reproduced on page 37 of this publication) is considered by experts to be a first-class building in every particular, one that will prove entirely satisfactory to the tax payers and citizens of Cook County. This building has been standing all of the past winter without a roof without causing the least injury or settling in any part of the building. This may be accepted as conclusive proof of the solid character of the foundation and superstructure.

LOWEST CUT RATES TO ALL PARTS OF THE WORLD

AT THE J. A. Webb Company

RAILROAD TICKET BROKERS

153 South Clark St. Tel. Main 3895.

M. R. LEYDEN. ESTABLISHED 1868. R. J. COLLINS.

LEYDEN & COLLINS

Commission Merchants and Wholesale Meat Dealers

Butter, Eggs, Veal, Poultry, Hogs, Mutton, Beef, Hides, Tallow, Etc. COOLING ROOMS.

Nos. 10 & 12 Fulton Street Wholesale Market, Chicago.

TELEPHONE MAIN 4599.

STORE NO GOODS UNTIL YOU GET OUR RATES

CLEAN, DRY, WELL VENTILATED ROOMS WITH KEY.

ESTIMATES FURNISHED. **STORAGE** TELEPHONE ENGLEWOOD 45.

BOXING, CRATING, PACKING, SHIPPING AND **MOVING** OF FURNITURE AND PIANOS OUR SPECIALTY.

BAGGAGE CALLED FOR AND DELIVERED TO ALL PARTS OF THE CITY.

ECONOMICAL STORAGE CO. 637, 639 AND 641 WEST SIXTY-THIRD STREET.

TRUNKS OR BICYCLES STORED AT ONE CENT PER DAY. MONEY ADVANCED.

The A. E. Schreiber Iron Works

TELEPHONE WEST 643

156-158 W. Ohio St., Cor. Morgan

MANUFACTURERS OF

Structural and Ornamental Iron Work

JAIL AND STAIR WORK.

ADAM M. SCHILLO

Livery, Boarding and Sale Stables

Carriages, Busses, Etc., at Reasonable Rates.
Horse Boarding a Specialty.

NOS. 367 TO 371 EAST NORTH AVENUE, CHICAGO.

TELEPHONE NORTH 107.

THE MAGIC WHEEL OF '96

WHY DID THE

DAYTON WHEEL

BOOM SO SUDDENLY IN AMERICA?

FIRST—It was the first to use large tubing for the main frame.

SECOND—It proved itself Stiffer, Stronger, Faster and Handsomer than all competitors.

THIRD—It was not placed on the market until fully perfected and tested by the best bicycle experts, who pronounce it the finest wheel ever built.

FOURTH—The best and most complete line of strictly high-grade Gents'and Ladies' Wheels, Racers, Tandems and Triplets ever shown by any manufacturer in this country.

THE DAYTON has revolutionized bicycle construction of '96. Visit Dayton Sales Parlors, most elegant in city, 340 Wabash Ave. Branch, 74 Washington St.

Davis Sewing Machine Co...Makers.

www.ingramcontent.com/pod-product-compliance
Lightning Source LLC
Chambersburg PA
CBHW020551270326
41927CB00006B/795